RECORDED VERSIONS GUITAR®

AUTHENTIC TRANSCRIPTIONS WITH NOTES AND TABLATURE

S0-BWF-369

Lilith Fair

A Celebration of Women in Music

Introduction ©1998 Madrigal Press Ltd.
Reprinted courtesy of Madrigal Press.
Contact: books@madrigalpress.com

www.lilithfair.com
www.nettwerk.com

Music transcriptions by Pete Billmann, Jeff Jacobson, Troy Nelson, Jeff Perrin, Matt Scharfglass, Jeffrey Story, and Dave Whitehill

Back cover photo by Brian Minato

ISBN 0-7935-9748-4X

HAL•LEONARD®
CORPORATION

7777 W. BLUEMOUND RD. P.O. BOX 13819 MILWAUKEE, WI 53213

Visit Hal Leonard Online at
www.halleonard.com

Lilith

Celebration of w

Sarah McLachlan

Introduction

Lilith Fair is one of the most meaningful and joyous events to occur in my life and it's something I'm very proud to be a part of. In being the spokesperson for **Lilith**, I've learned so much – not only about myself, but about the ever-changing and evolving attitudes towards women in our society.

Lilith Fair has been praised as being a turning point for women in music. I prefer to think of it as an ongoing progression. The summer festivals out there were completely male dominated even though there was a wealth of great and diverse music being made by women. This made no sense to me – why were we all lumped into one category of women's music? Why weren't we all regarded as unique and talented human beings? My reasons for **Lilith** were not wholly a reaction, yet these realities were part of the path towards its inception.

So, Lilith Fair was created for many reasons: the joy of sharing live music; the connection of like minds; the desire to create a sense of community that I felt was lacking in our industry... I did this with innocence, I did this with the desire to make things better. I think music has that gift – to give hope, to bring people to an elevated state of mind, to connect.

To all the artists who appeared on **Lilith Fair** and to all the music lovers out there... Thank you.

Peace and Love,

(Excerpted from the foreword From Lilith to Lilith Fair by Buffy Childerhose)

Mississippi

Words and Music by Paula Cole

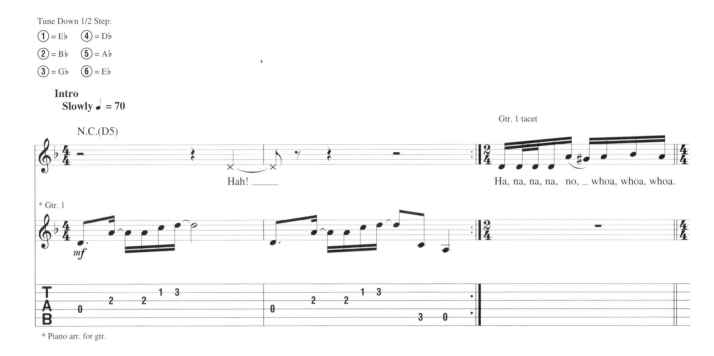

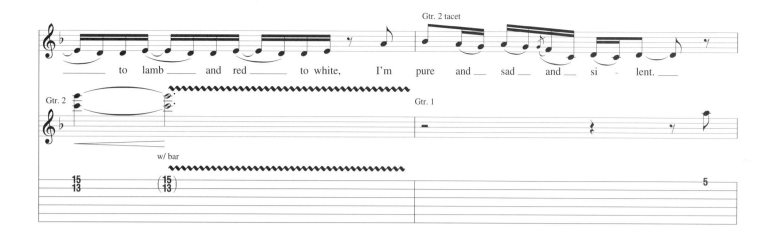

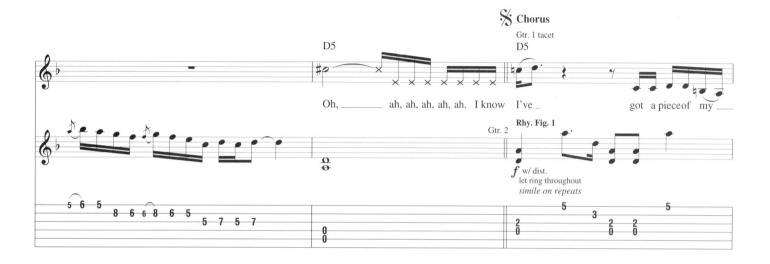

*Chord symbols reflect overall tonality.

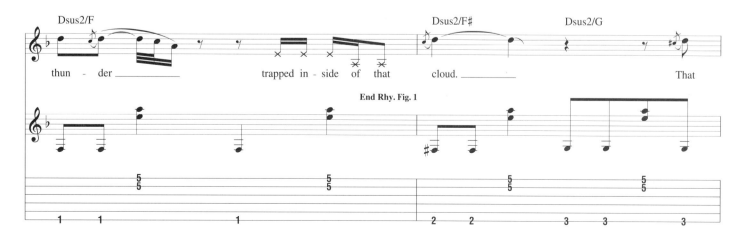

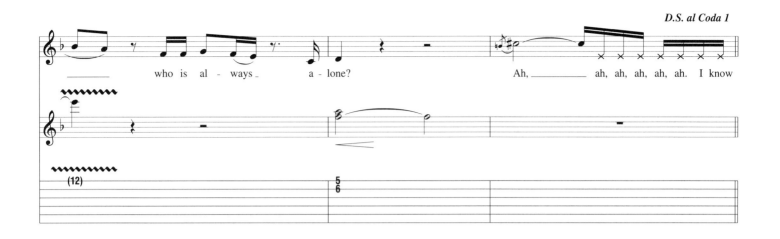

who is al - ways _ a - lone? Ah, _____ ah, ah, ah, ah, ah. I know

⊕ Coda 1

Interlude
D5

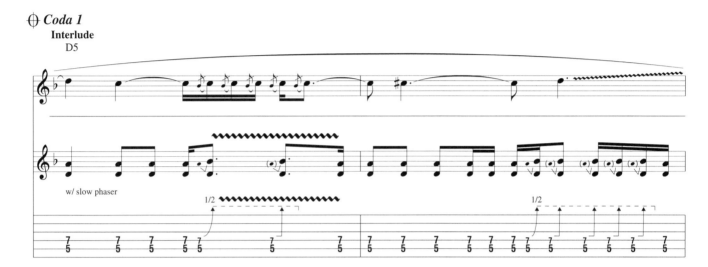

w/ slow phaser

Bridge
Gtr. 2 tacet
C   G

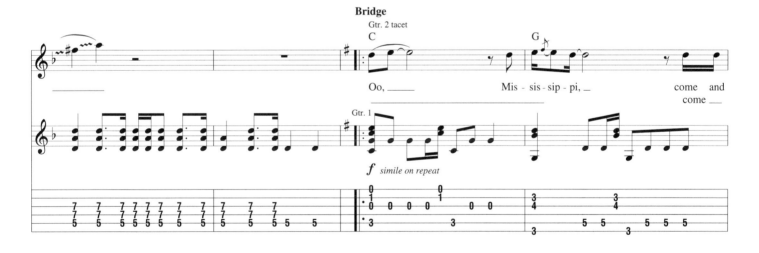

Oo, _____ Mis - sis - sip - pi, _____ come and
come _____

f simile on repeat
Gtr. 1

F   G

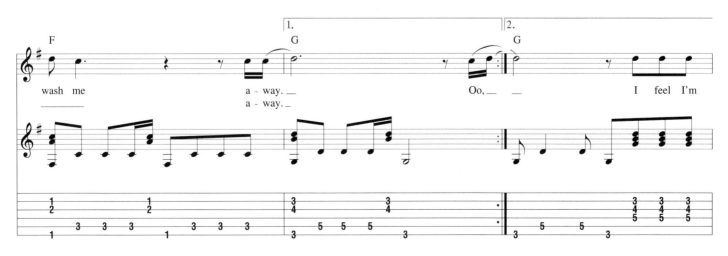

wash me   a - way. _
a - way. _
Oo, _ _   I feel I'm

1.
2.   G

Scooter Boys

Words and Music by Amy Ray

Drop D Tuning:
① = E ④ = D
② = B ⑤ = A
③ = G ⑥ = D

Chorus
Free Time

Moderately ♩ = 109

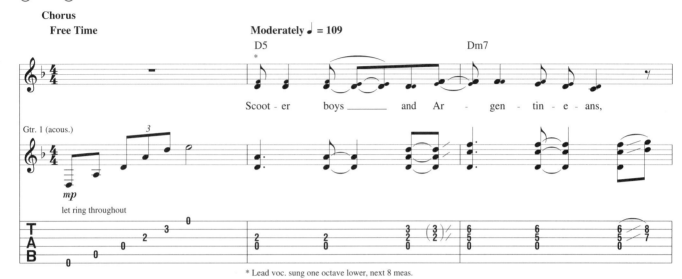

Scoot- er boys _____ and Ar- gen- ti- ne- ans,

* Lead voc. sung one octave lower, next 8 meas.

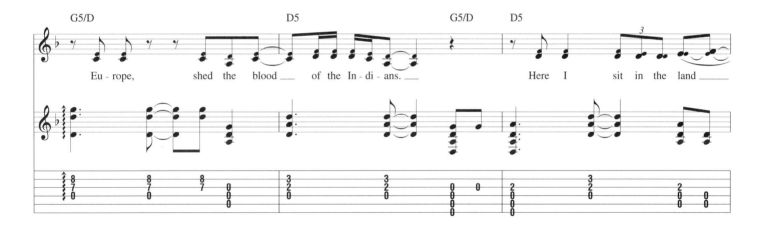

Eu- rope, shed the blood _____ of the In- di- ans. _____ Here I sit in the land _____

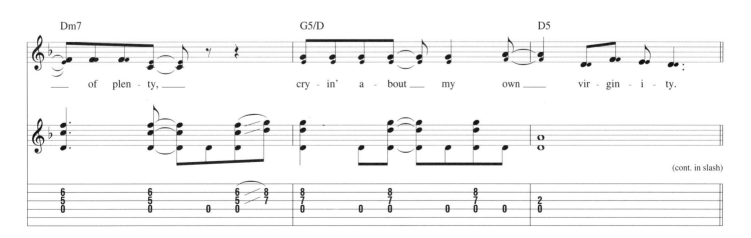

_____ of plen- ty, _____ cry- in' a- bout _____ my own _____ vir- gin- i- ty.

(cont. in slash)

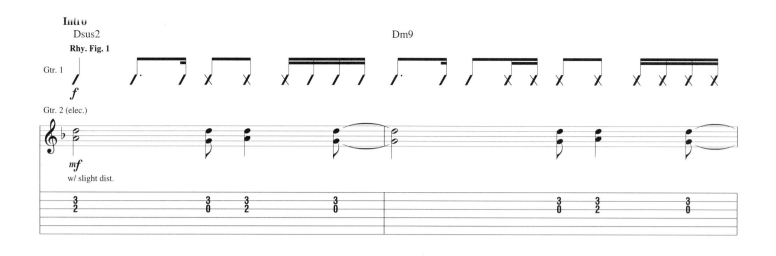

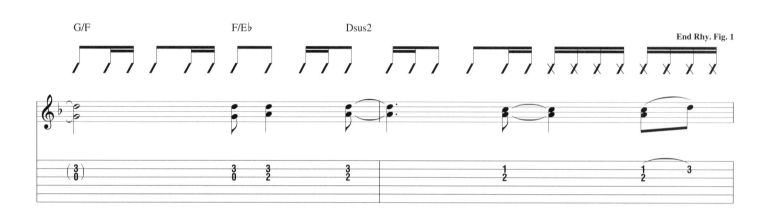

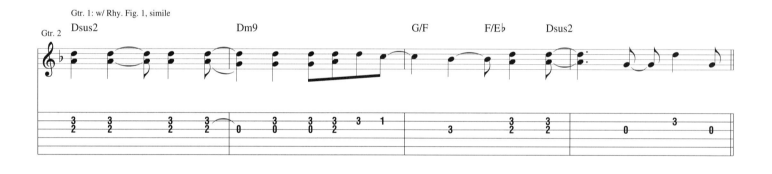

Verse

1. Hey, blue blood, you're noth-in' new. __ You see, I come __ from priv-

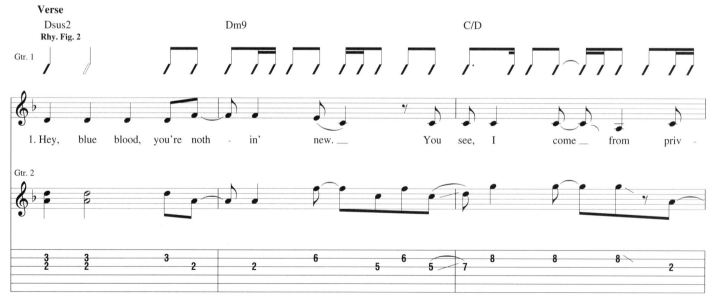

Gtr. 1: w/ Rhy. Fig. 2, simile

Dsus2   Dsus2   Dm9

'lege, too. It's a   chap - ter in the book   on ____ the A - mer - i - cas and

C/D   Dsus2   Chorus   Dsus2

you're just an - oth - er co - lo - ni - al ter - or - ist. Scoot - er boys ____ and Ar -

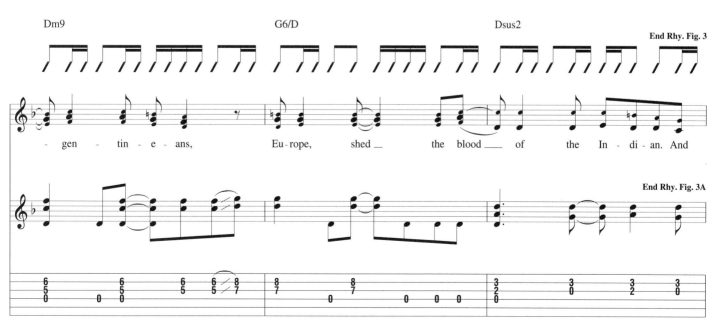

Dm9   G6/D   Dsus2

- gen - tin - e - ans, Eu - rope, shed ____ the blood ____ of the In - di - an. And

here I sit in the land of plen-ty, _____ cry-in' a-bout _____ my own _____ vir-gin-i-ty.

Interlude

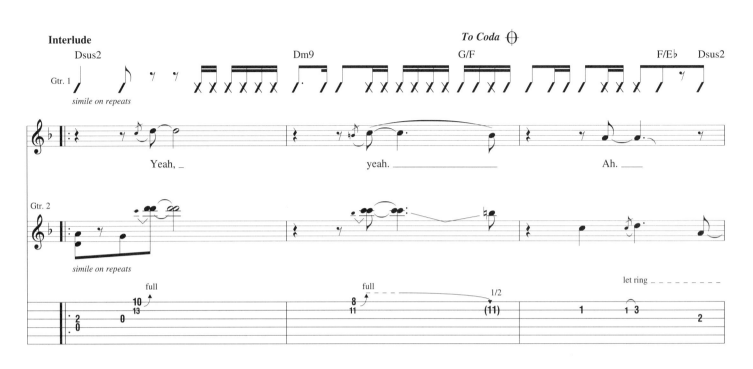

Yeah, _____ yeah. _____ Ah. _____

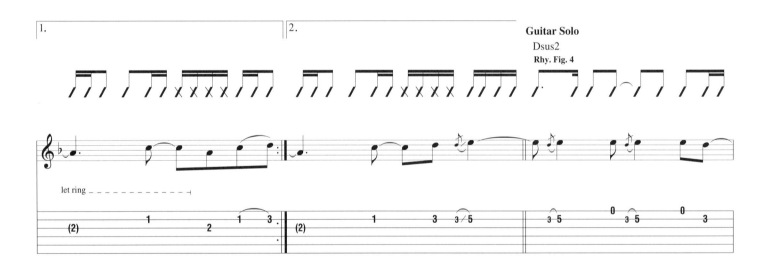

Guitar Solo

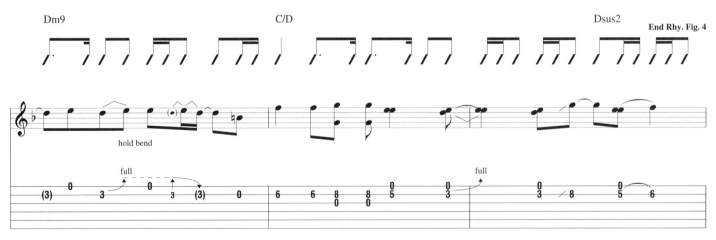

steal - in' from the best to feed the poor." Well, they need ___ more. The

Coda

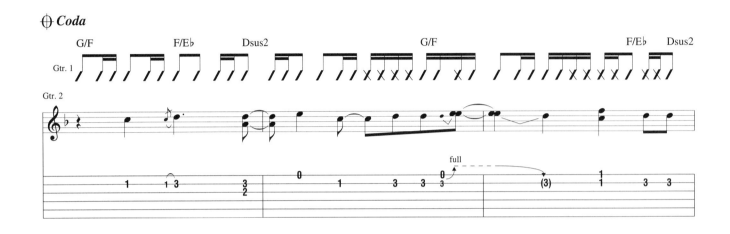

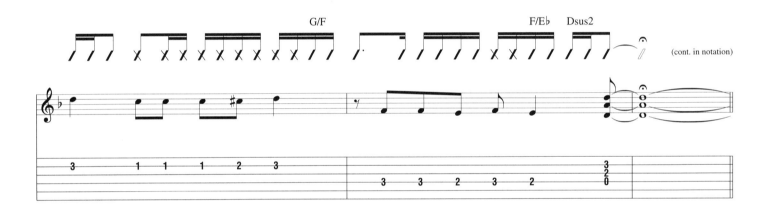

Outro

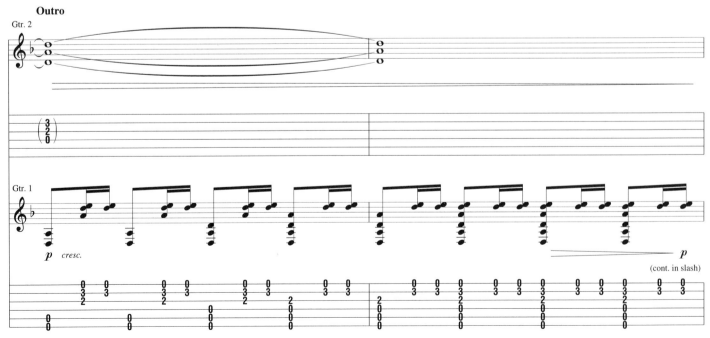

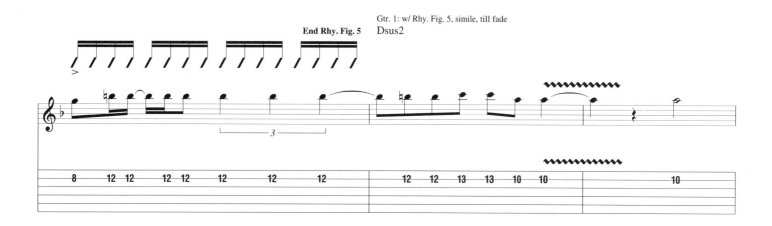

Been It

Music by Peter Svensson
Lyrics by Nina Persson and Peter Svensson

I Want

Words and Music by Dayna Manning

Additional Lyrics

3. I want to sleep for hours and hours.
   I want a garden full of beautiful sunflowers.
   I want to go to be seen.
   And I want to be friends with Tom Petty.

4. I want someone to grant my wishes.
   I want a boy who'll blow me kisses.
   I want a friend that I can care for.
   And I want to find a love that's not so paintful.

Four Leaf Clover

Words and Music by Abra Moore

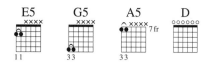

Gtr. 1; Open D Tuning:
① = D ④ = D
② = A ⑤ = A
③ = F♯ ⑥ = D

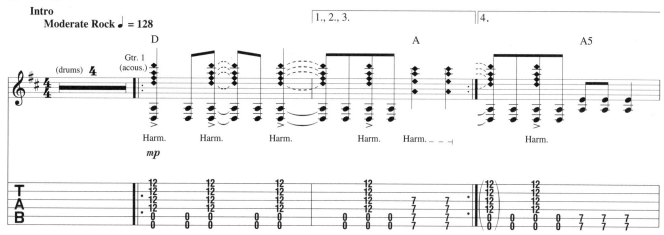

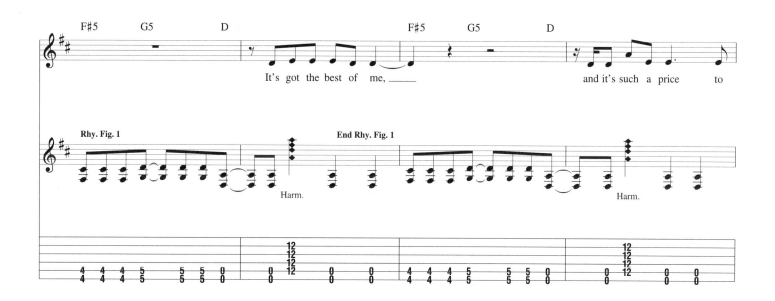

It's got the best of me, _____ and it's such a price to pay. Well, it's got the best of me. _____ 1. See, I've _____

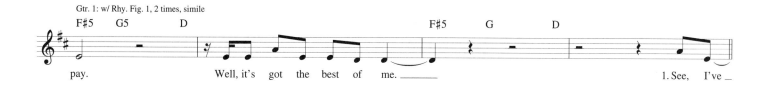

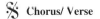

Chorus/ Verse

Gtr. 2: w/ Rhy. Fill 1, 2nd, 3rd & 4th times
Gtr. 2: w/ Rhy. Fill 3, 4 times, 5th time

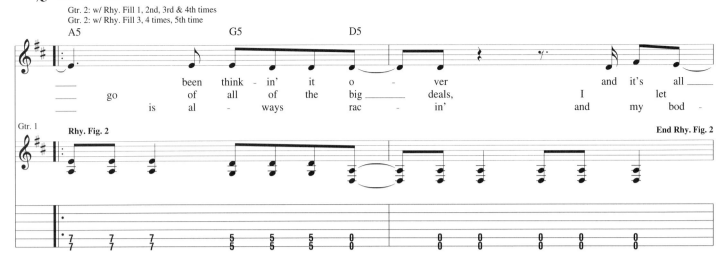

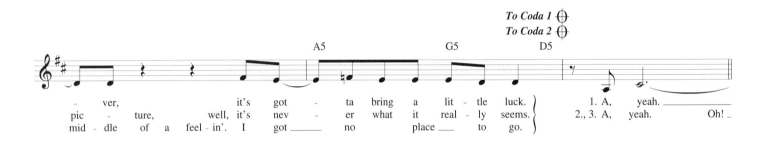

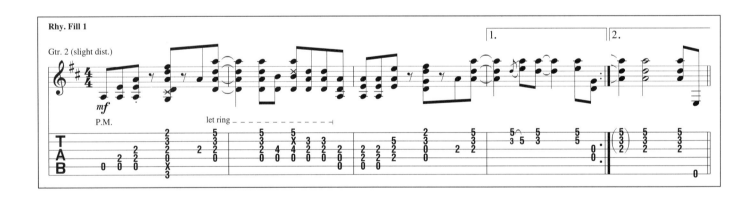

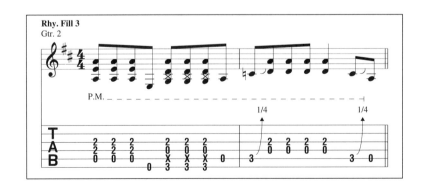

24

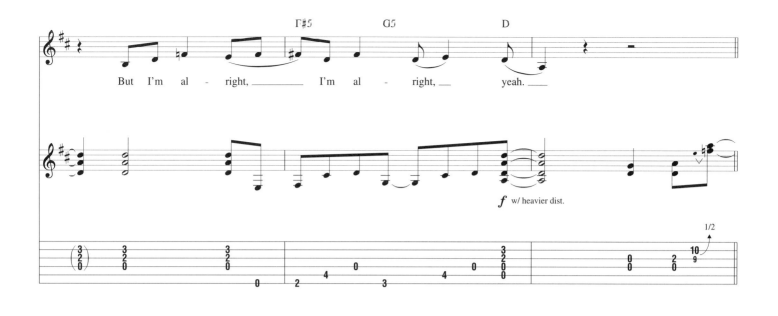

But I'm al - right, _____ I'm al - right, _____ yeah. _____

Guitar Solo

Gtr. 1: w/ Rhy. Fig. 2, 12 times, simile

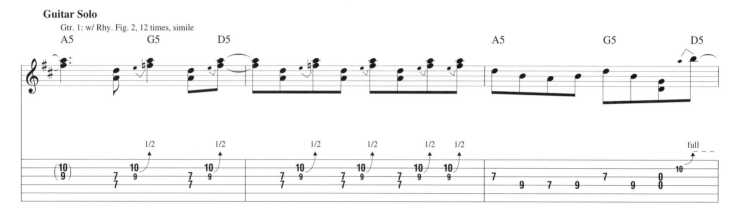

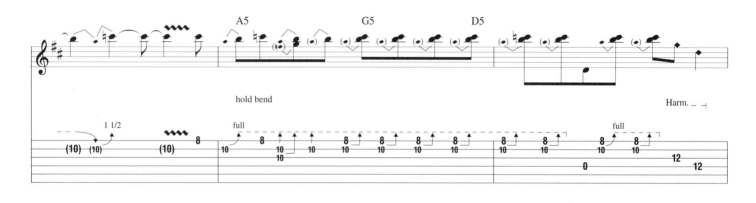

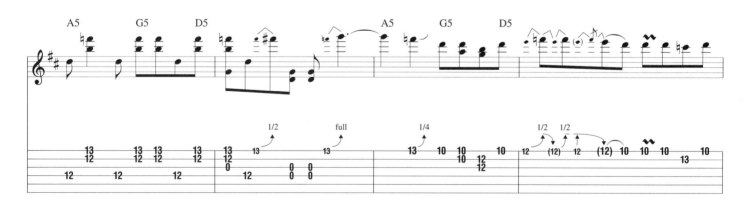

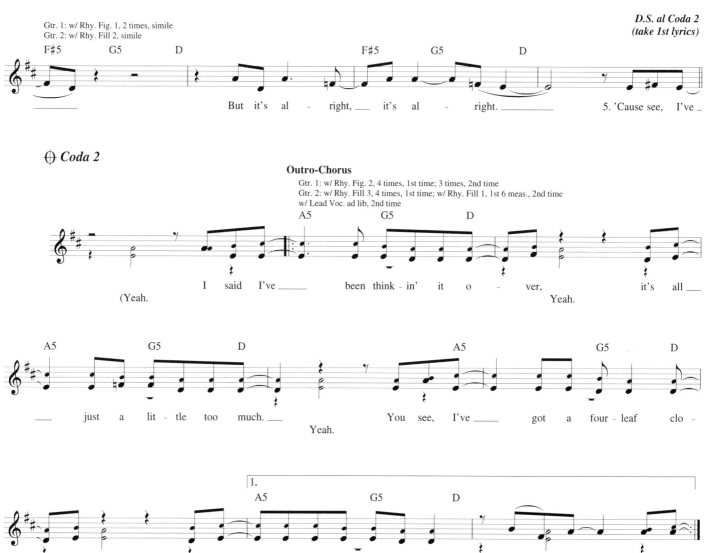

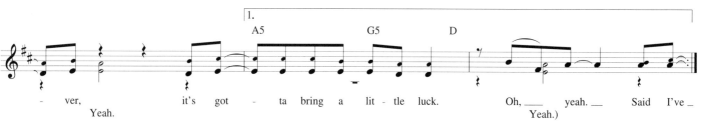

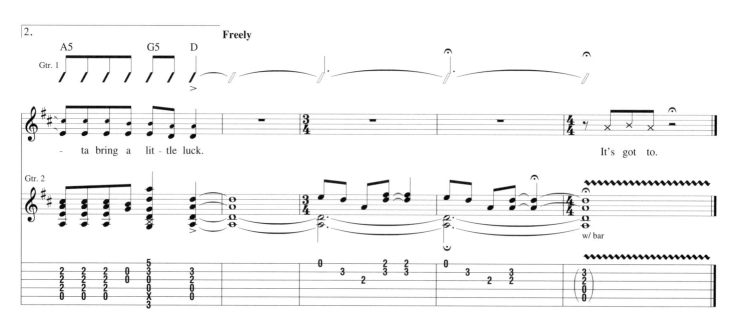

Falling in Love

Words and Music by Lisa Loeb

Capo II

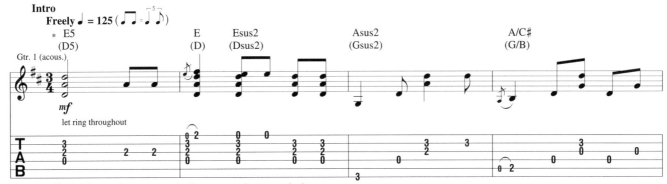

*Symbols in parentheses represent chord names respective to capoed guitar.
Symbols above reflect actual sounding chords. Capoed fret is "0" in TAB.

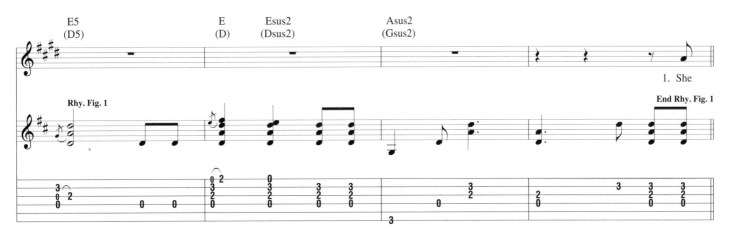

1. She

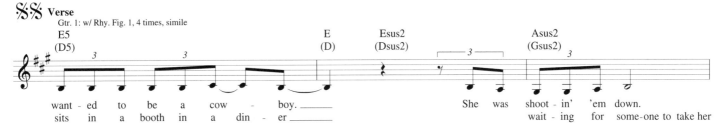

want- ed   to   be   a   cow- boy. _____   She   was   shoot- in'   'em   down.
sits   in   a   booth   in   a   din- er _____   wait- ing   for   some-one   to   take   her

or- der,   She   was   tramp- in'   a- round.
wait- ing   for   some-one   to   come   and   sit   down.

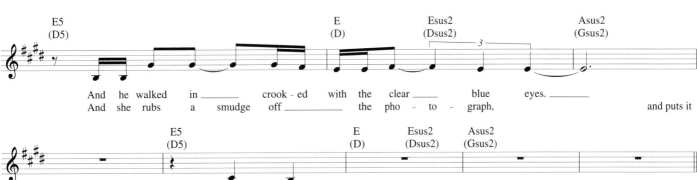

And   he   walked   in _____   crook- ed   with   the   clear _____   blue   eyes.
And   she   rubs   a   smudge   off _____   the   pho- to- graph,   and   puts   it

back _   in-to   her   purse.   Mm. _____

Well, the

Loneliness of the Long Distance Runner

Words and Music by Shannon Worrell

1. Keep - ing a - part _____ to stay ___ to - geth - er. _____
2. Tear - drops split, di - vid - ed _____ in - to stars. _____

You are a bell _____ that should _ be ring - ing, o - ver hill ____
Will we for - give _____ our - selves ___ for all _ we're not, ___ all ____

____ and Heath - er. _____ You are the bell _____ that broke _ the world.
____ we are. _____ With an ___ arm ___ out in _ the dark. _____

_____ I'm hap - py to know ___ you, I _____ guess,
_____ Hold - ing still, ___ is still ___ the

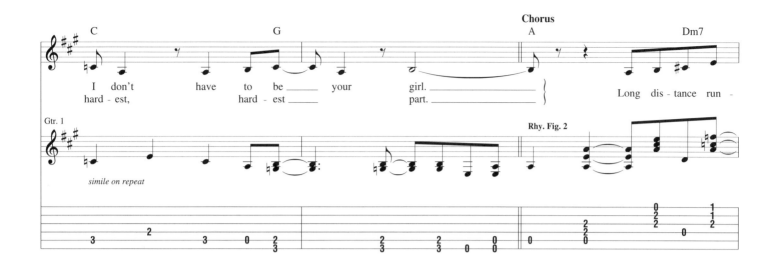

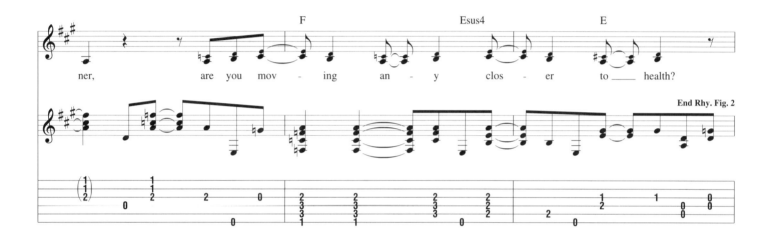

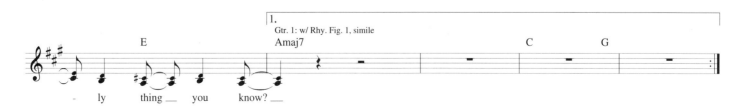

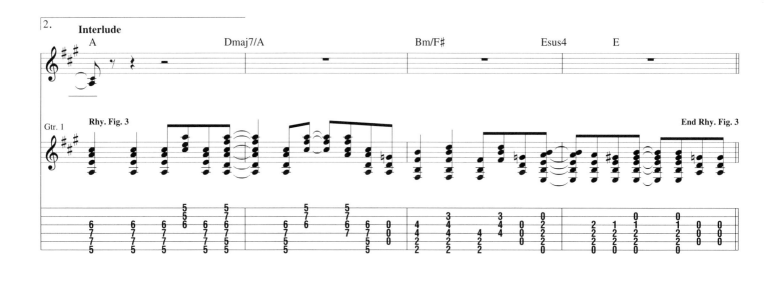

Bridge

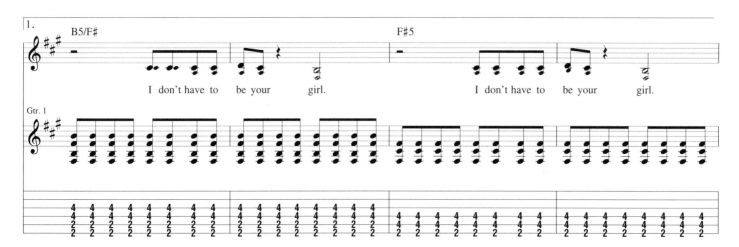

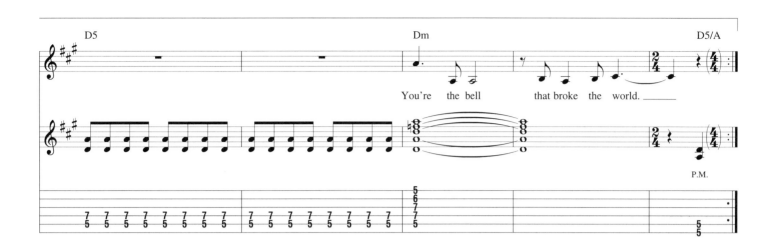

You're the bell that broke the world. _____

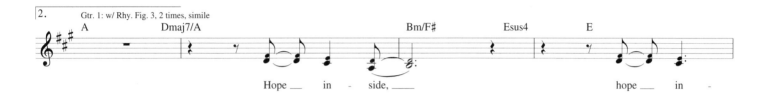

Hope _____ in - side, _____ hope _____ in -

side.

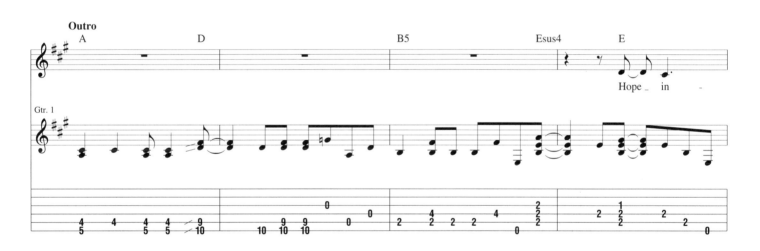

Hope _____ in -

side.

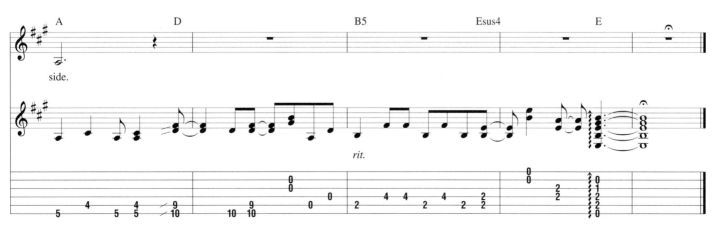

Eternal Flame

Words and Music by Billy Steinberg, Tom Kelly and Susanna Hoffs

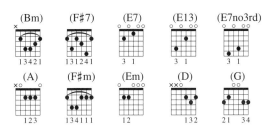

Gtrs. 1 & 2: Capo IV

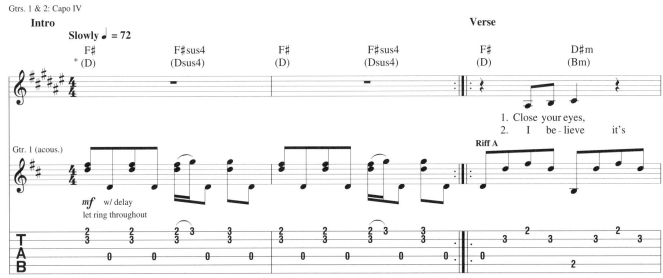

* Symbols in parentheses represent chord names respective to capoed guitar.
  Symbols above reflect actual sounding chord. Capoed fret is "0" in TAB.

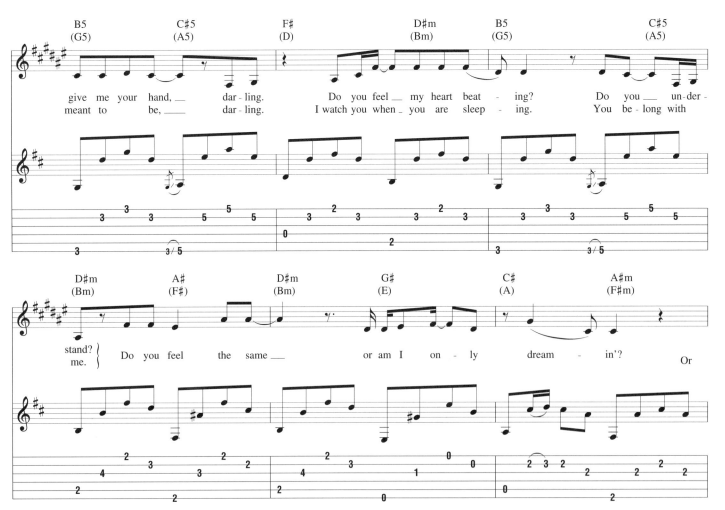

Guitar Solo

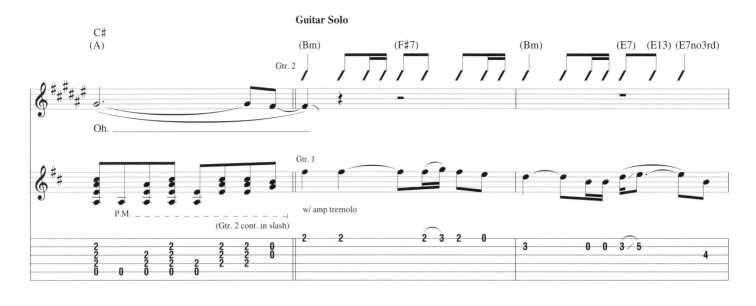

D.S. al Coda

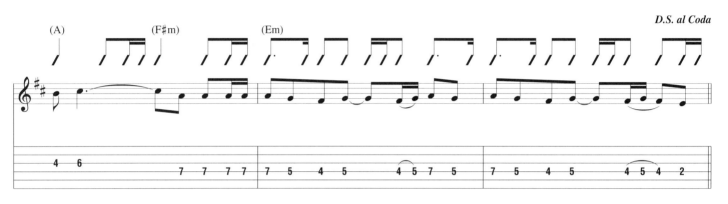

⊕ Coda

Verse
Gtr. 1: w/ Riff A

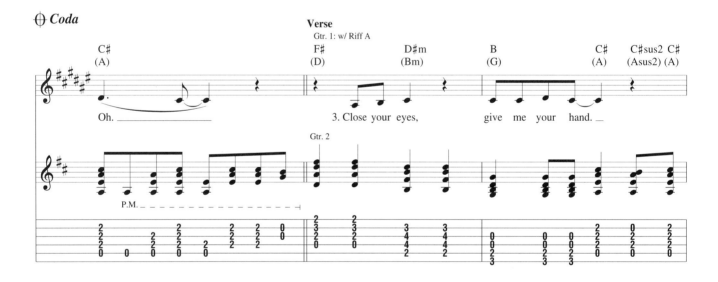

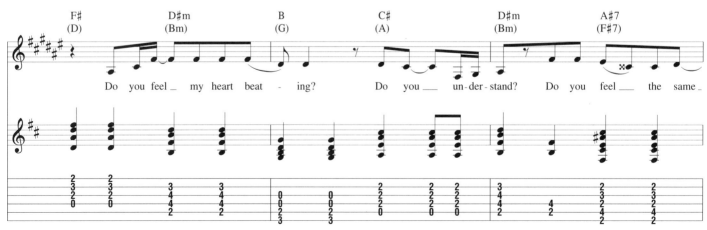

Rock in This Pocket (Song of David)

Words and Music by Suzanne Vega

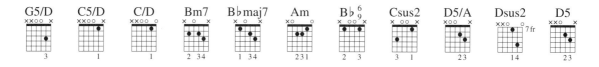

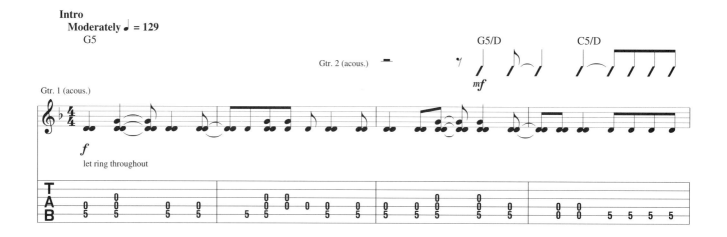

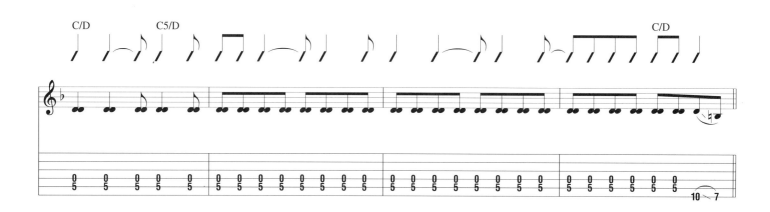

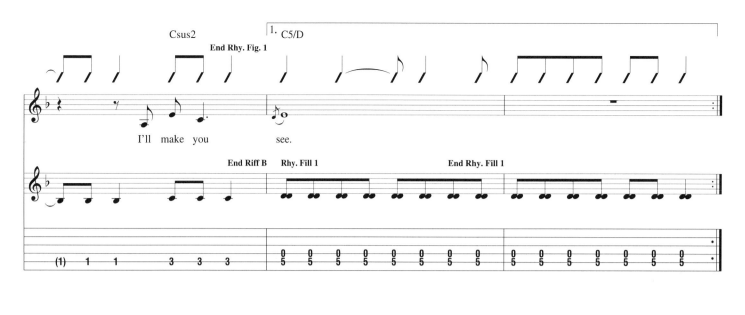

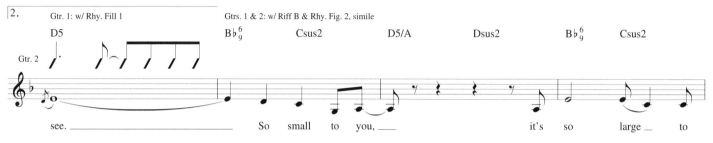

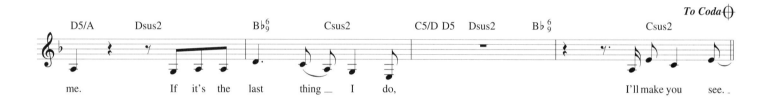

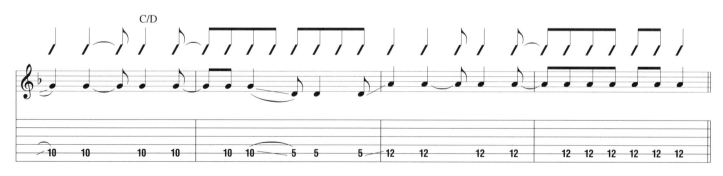

Verse

Gtrs. 1 & 2: w/ Riff A & Rhy. Fig. 1, 9 times, simile

3. I might be out like a light ex - tin - guished in the throw.

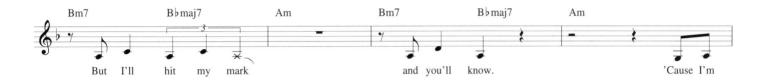

But I'll hit my mark and you'll know. 'Cause I'm

real - ly well ac - quaint - ed with the span of your ___ brow. ___

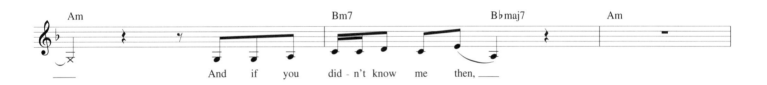

___ And if you did - n't know me then, ___

D.S. al Coda
(take 2nd ending)

you'll know me now, ___ you'll know me now. ___ And what's

⊕ Coda

Make you see, ___ make you see. ___

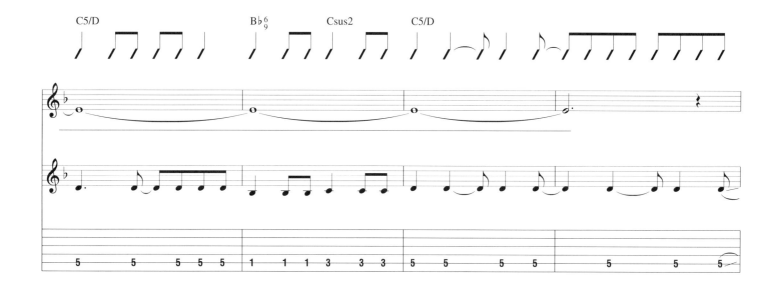

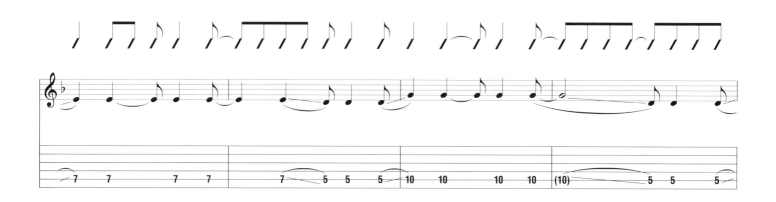

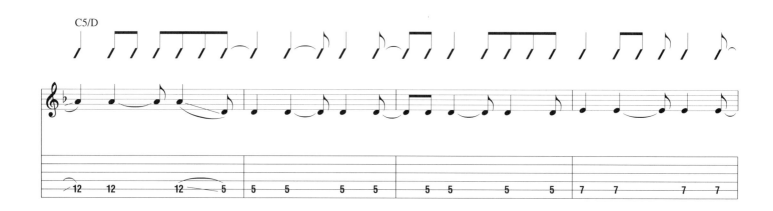

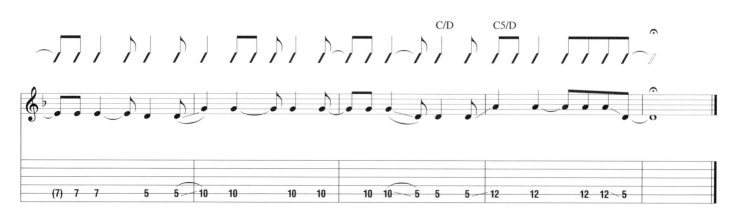

Ladder

Words and Music by Joan Osborne, Rick Chertoff, Eric Bazilian and Rob Hyman

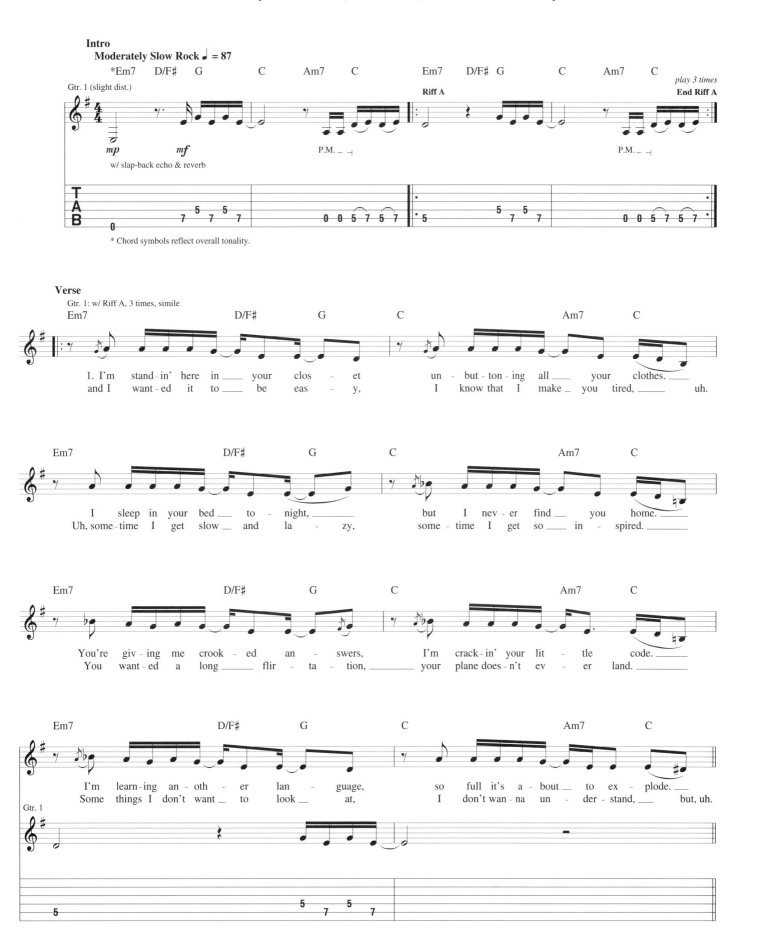

Pre-Chorus

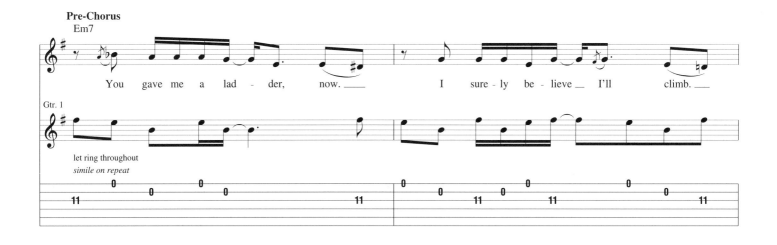

You gave me a lad - der, now. ____ I sure-ly be-lieve __ I'll climb. ____

Gtr. 1

let ring throughout
simile on repeat

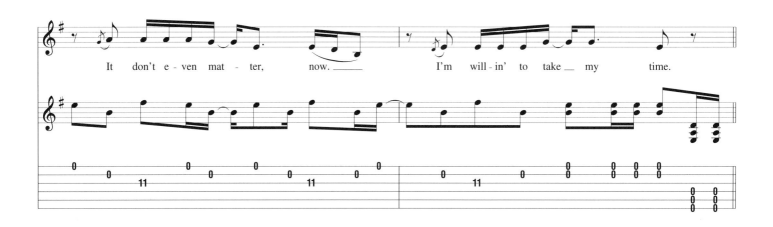

It don't e-ven mat-ter, now. ____ I'm will-in' to take __ my time.

Chorus

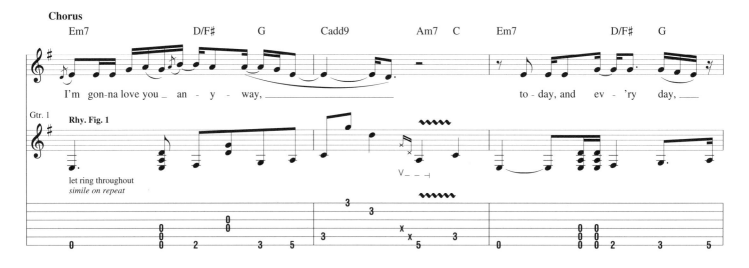

I'm gon-na love you __ an - y - way, ____ to - day, and ev - 'ry day, ____

Gtr. 1

Rhy. Fig. 1

let ring throughout
simile on repeat

to - day and ev - 'ry day. I'm gon-na love you __ an - y - way, ____ my, ____

End Rhy. Fig. 1

rake ┘

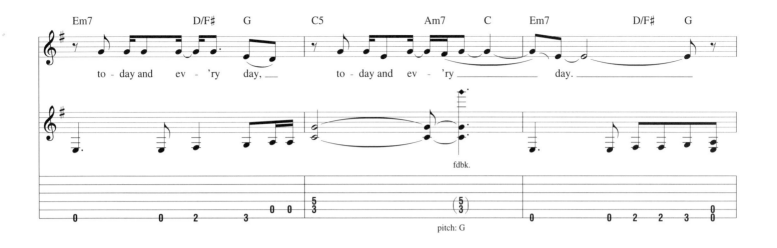

to - day and ev - 'ry day, ___ to - day and ev - 'ry _____ day. _____

fdbk.

pitch: G

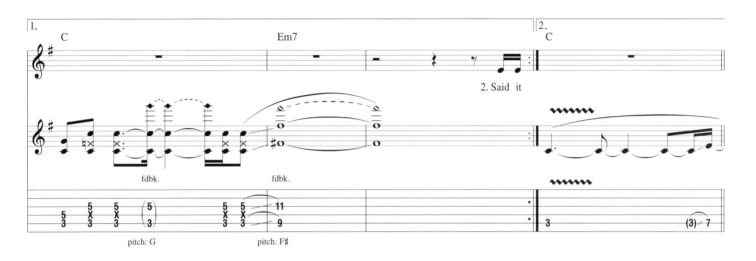

1.   C   Em7   2.   C

2. Said it

fdbk.   fdbk.

pitch: G   pitch: F#

Interlude

w/ Bkgd. Voc. ad lib.

E5

pitch: B   G#   B   F#

Bridge

E5   Em6   Em7   Em6   Em7

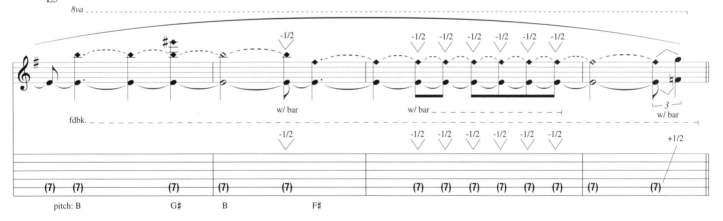

You   gave   me   a   lad - der,   now. _____   I   sure - ly   be - lieve __   I'll   climb. _____

loco

let ring throughout

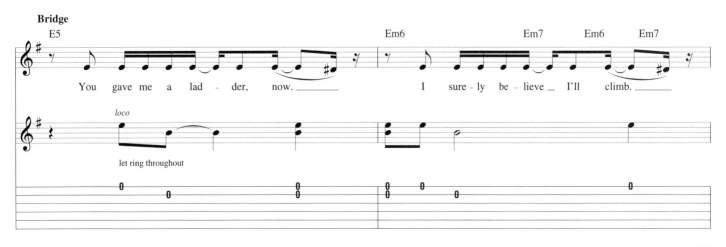

pitch: A

pitch: A

Outro-Chorus

Gtr. 1: w/ Rhy. Fig. 1, 4 times, simile

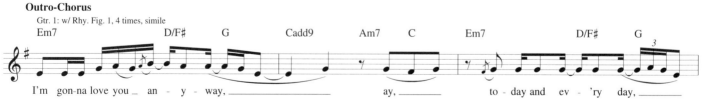

to - day and ev - 'ry day. _____ I'm gon - na love you ___ an - y - way, _____

_____ to - day and ev - 'ry day, _____ to - day and ev - 'ry _____

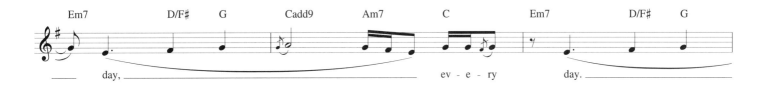

___ day, _____ ev - e - ry day. _____

_____ To - day and ev - 'ry day, _____ to - day and ev - 'ry day. _____

To - day and ev - 'ry, ev - 'ry, ev - 'ry, ev - 'ry, ev - 'ry, ev - 'ry

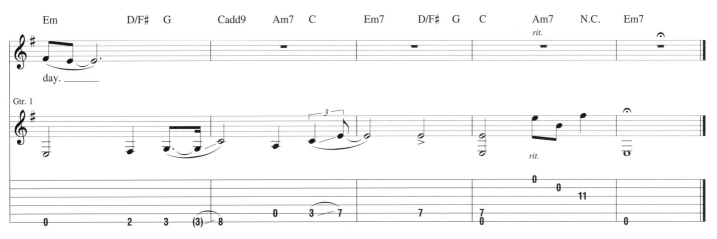

day. _____

Gtr. 1

Building a Mystery

Words and Music by Sarah McLachlan and Pierre Marchand

Verse

Gtr. 1: w/ Rhy. Fig. 1, 4 times, simile
Gtr. 1: w/ Rhy. Fill 1, 2nd time
Gtr. 1: w/ Rhy. Fig. 1, last meas., 2nd time, simile

Bm (Em)   G/D (C/G)   D (G)   A/E (D/A)

live in a church
- ing a - loud
where you sleep __ with voo - doo __ dolls, _____ and you
a prayer __ from your se - cret god _____ to

Gtr. 1: w/ Rhy. Fig. 1, 3 times, 2nd time, simile

Bm (Em)   G/D (C/G)   D (G)   A/E (D/A)

won't give up ___ the search ___
feed off of ___ fears _____
for the ghosts in the halls. _____
and hold back your tears, _____ oh. _____ You

Bm (Em)   G/D (C/G)   D (G)   A/E (D/A)

You wear san - dals in ___ the snow ___ and a
give us a tan - trum and a
smile __ I won't wash __ a - way. ___
know - it - all _____ grin, _____

Bm (Em)   G/D (C/G)   D (G)   A/E (D/A)

Can you look out the win - dow
just when you need one
with - out your ___ shad - ow get - ting in ___ the way? ___
when the eve - ning stayed. _____

Pre-Chorus

E5 (A5)   G/D (C/G)

You're so _____ beau - ti - ful,
You're a _____ beau - ti - ful,
(Oo, _____ ah, ___
with an edge and charm ___ - ing.
a beau - ti - ful fucked ___ up man. _
la. _

Gtr. 1

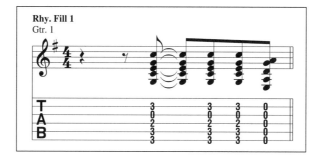

Rhy. Fill 1
Gtr. 1

Water Is Wide

(Traditional)
Arranged by Sarah McLachlan, Emily Saliers of the Indigo Girls and Jewel Kilcher

* Symbols in parentheses represent chord names respective to capoed guitars. Symbols above reflect actual sounding chord.
  Capoed fret is "0" in TAB. Chord symbols reflect basic tonality.

** composite arrangement

car - ry two.
and wax - es cold.

Then both _ shall _ row

way _____

my love _ and
like morn-ing

I. _____
dew. _____

To Coda ⊕

1.

2. Your love is gen -

2.

Guitar Solo

Gtr. 1

Gtr. 2

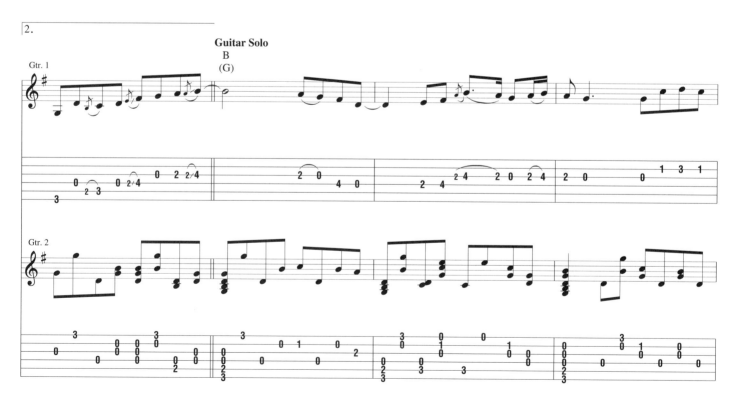

Additional Lyrics

3. Love is a ship that sails the sea,
   She's loaded deep, as deep can be.
   But not as deep as the love I'm in,
   And know not how I sink or swim.

Going Back to Harlan

Words and Music by Anna McGarrigle

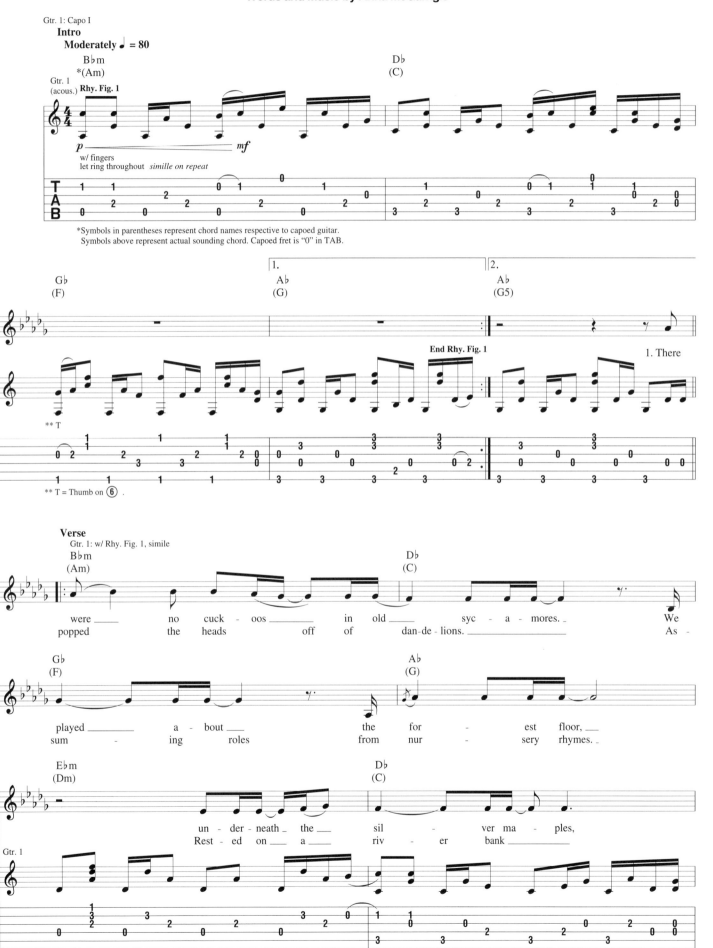

Gtr. 1: Capo I

*Symbols in parentheses represent chord names respective to capoed guitar.
Symbols above represent actual sounding chord. Capoed fret is "0" in TAB.

** T = Thumb on ⑥ .

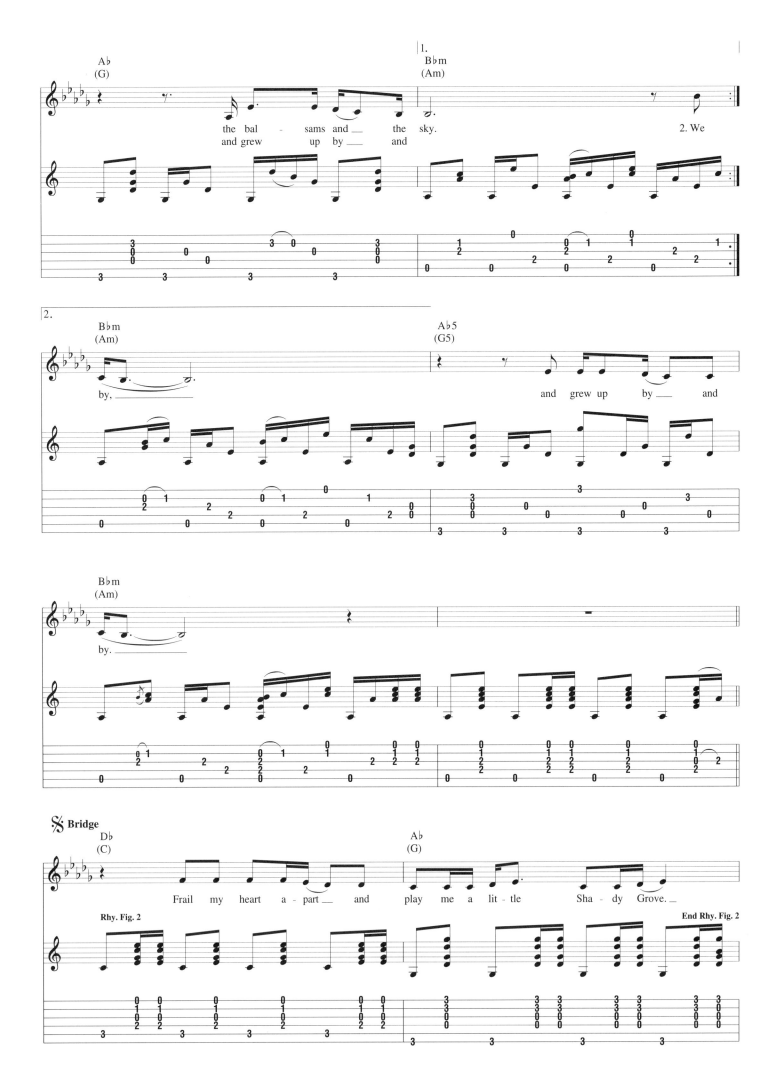

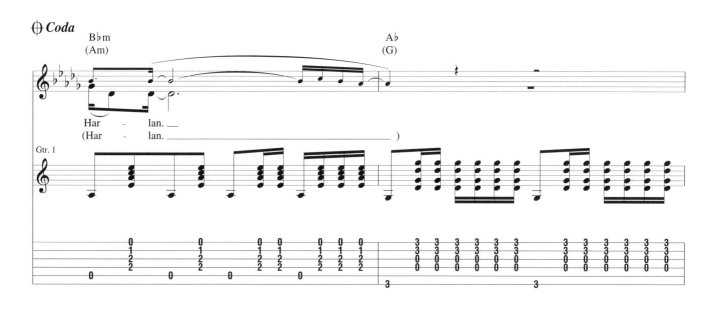

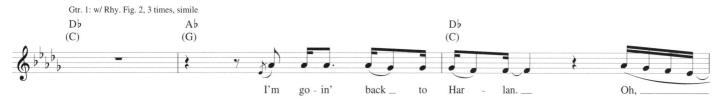

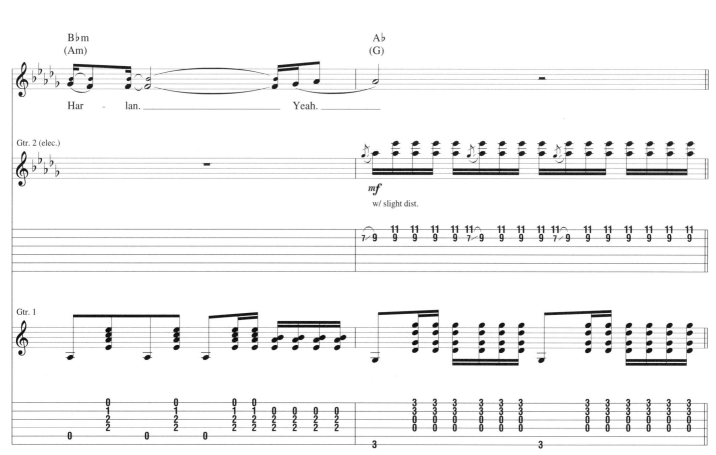

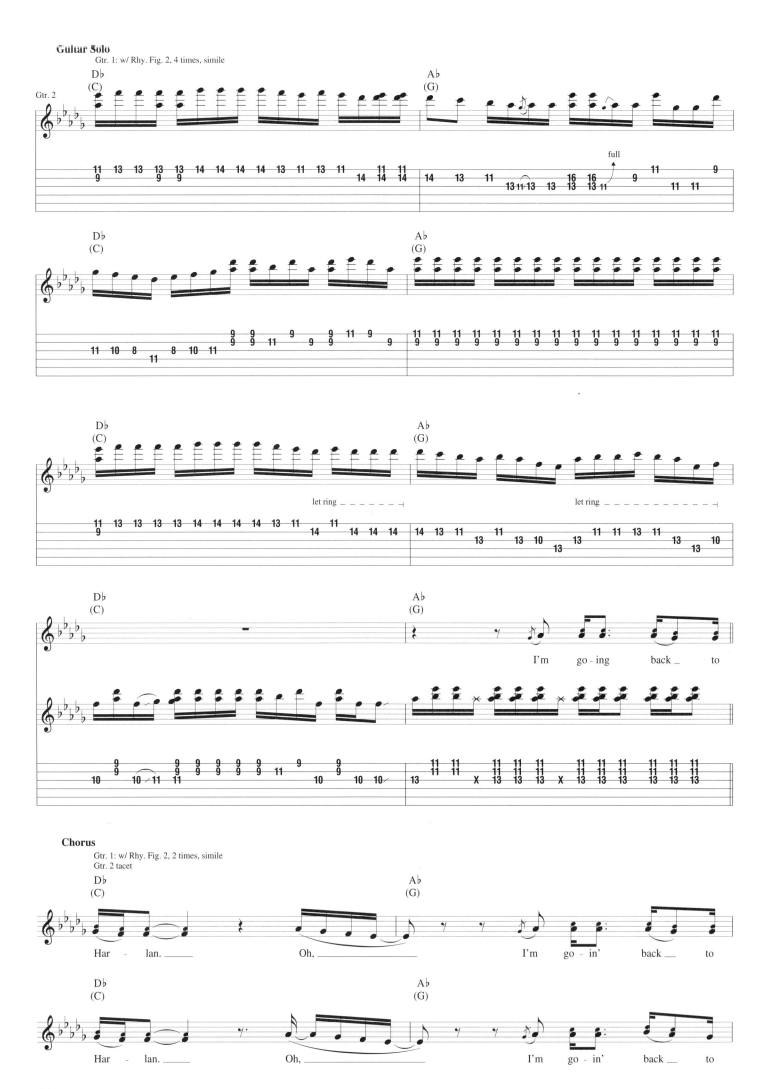

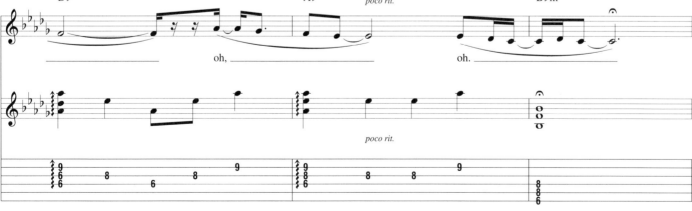

Wash My Hands

Words and Music by Meredith Brooks, Shelly Peiken and Larry Dvoskin

Pre-Chorus

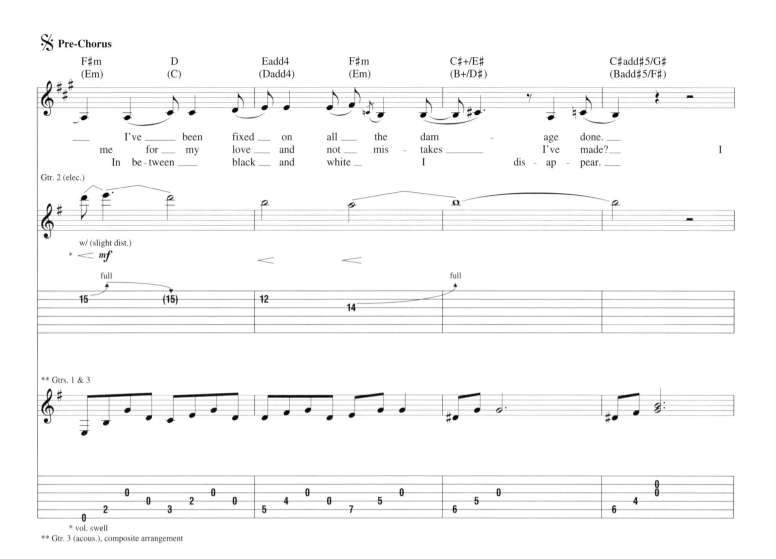

I've been fixed on all the dam - age done.
me for my love and not mis - takes I've made? I
In be - tween black and white I dis - ap - pear.

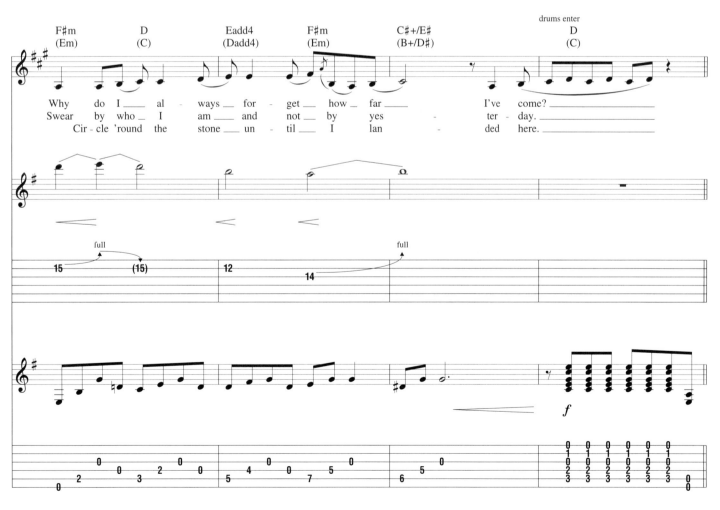

Why do I al - ways for - get how far I've come?
Swear by who I am and not by yes - ter - day.
Cir - cle 'round the stone un - til I lan - ded here.

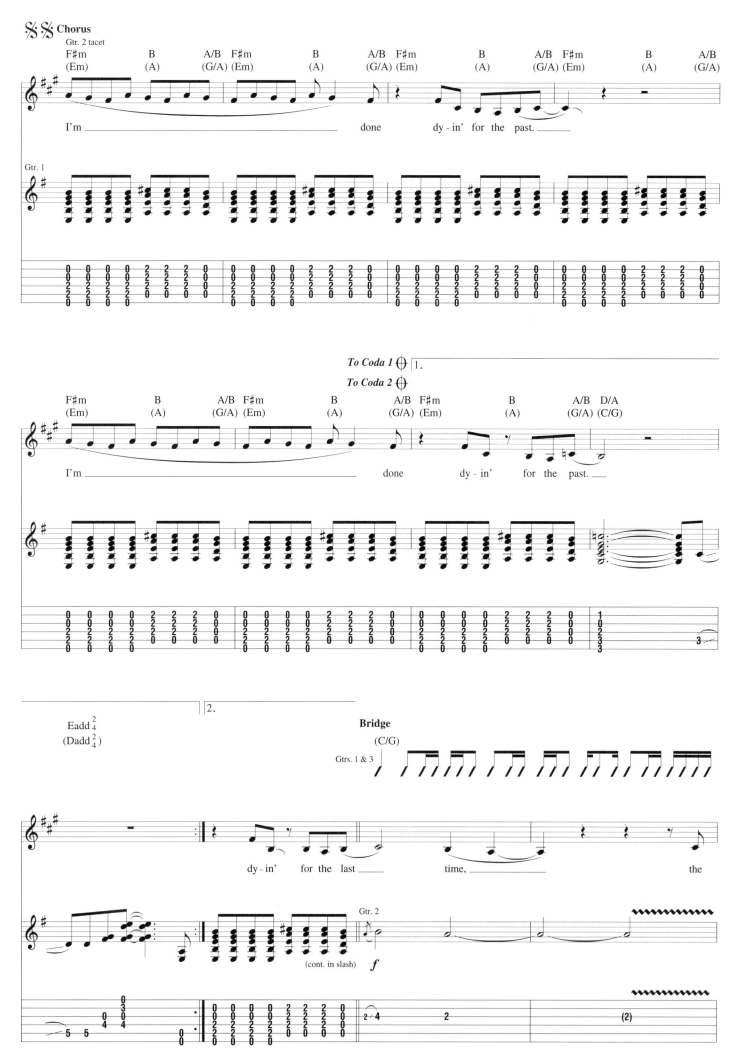

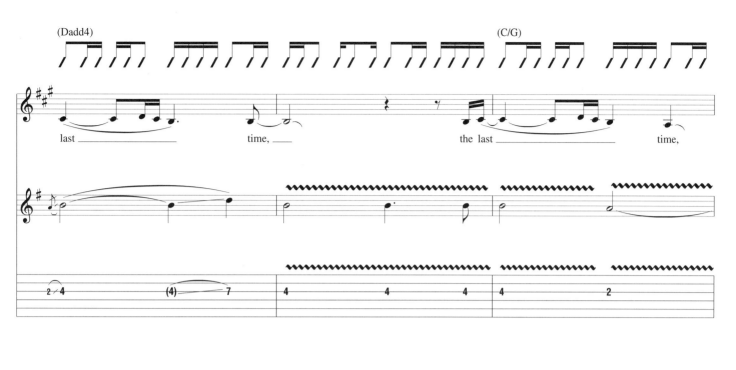

last _____ time, _____ the last _____ time,

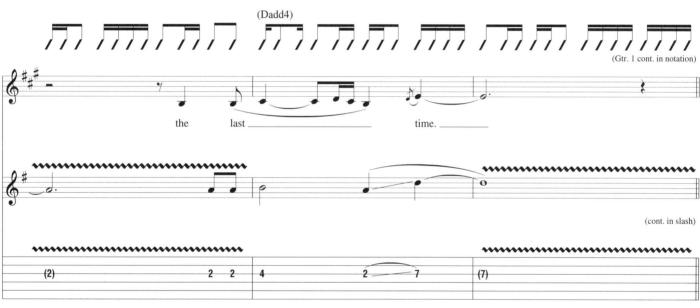

(Dadd4)

(Gtr. 1 cont. in notation)

the last _____ time. _____

(cont. in slash)

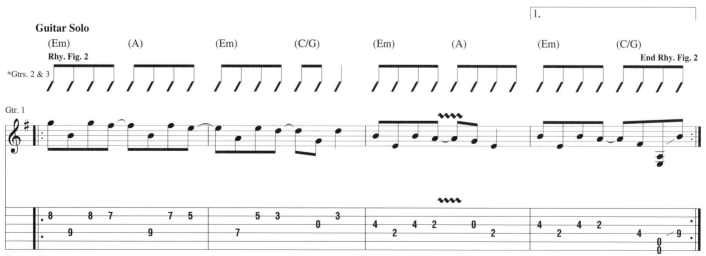

Guitar Solo

(Em)   (A)   (Em)   (C/G)   (Em)   (A)   (Em)   (C/G)

Rhy. Fig. 2   **End Rhy. Fig. 2**

*Gtrs. 2 & 3

Gtr. 1

* composite arrangement

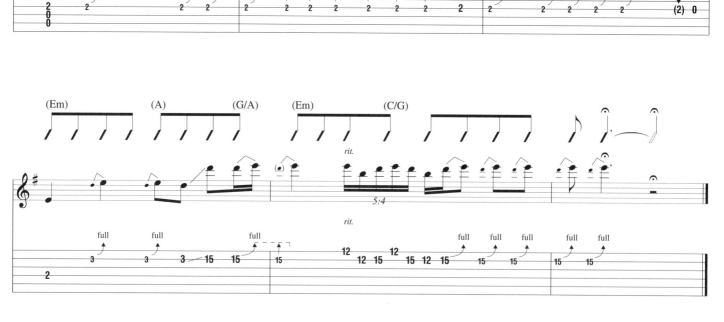

Cain

Words and Music by Patty Griffin

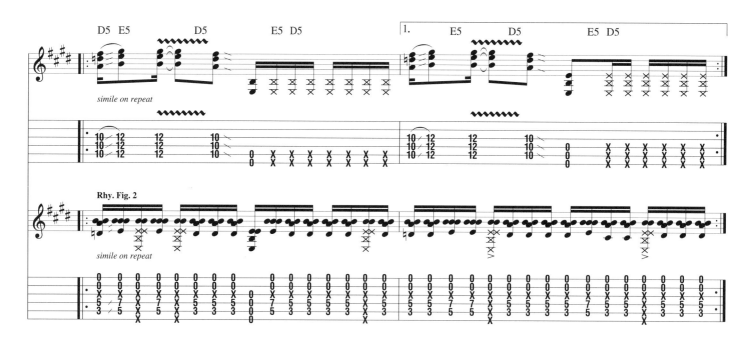

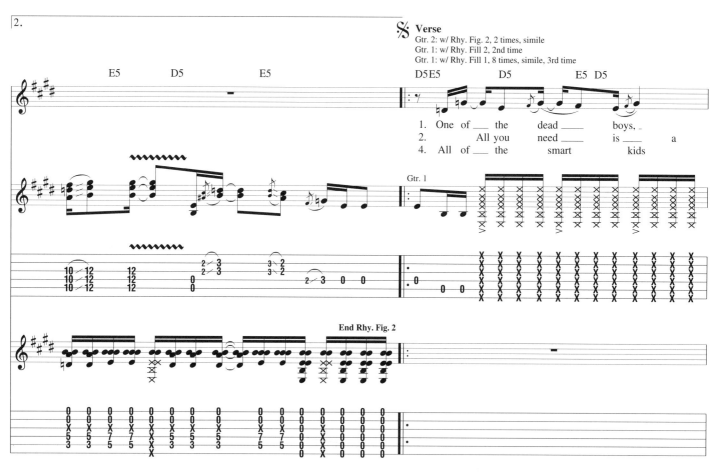

1. One of ___ the dead ___ boys, ___
2. ___ All you need ___ is ___ a
4. All of ___ the smart kids

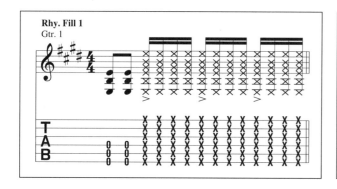

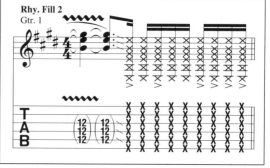

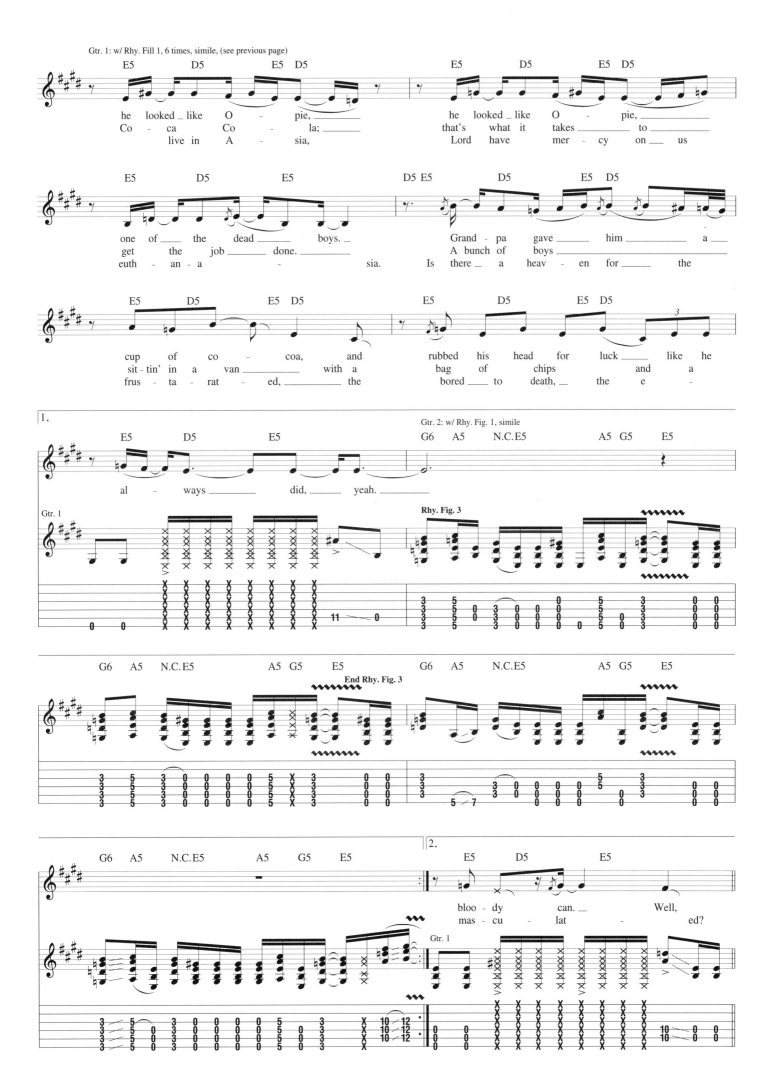

Chorus

Gtr. 1: w/ Rhy. Fig. 3, 2 times, simile
Gtr. 2: w/ Rhy. Fig. 1, simile

G6   A5   N.C. E5   A5 G5   E5   G6   A5   N.C. E5   A5 G5   E5

fath - er, do __ you know __ your son? __   Fath - er, do __ you know __ his name? __

To Coda ⊕

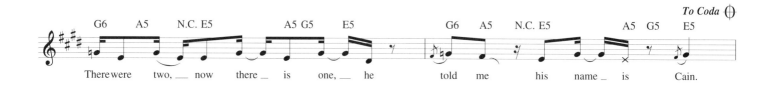

G6   A5   N.C. E5   A5 G5   E5   G6   A5   N.C. E5   A5 G5   E5

There were two, __ now there __ is one, __ he   told me   his name __ is Cain.

Gtr. 2: w/ Rhy. Fig. 2, simile
w/ Voc. ad lib. next 4 meas.

Gtr. 1

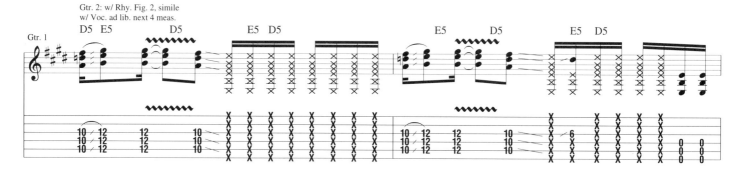

D5 E5   D5   E5 D5   E5   D5   E5 D5

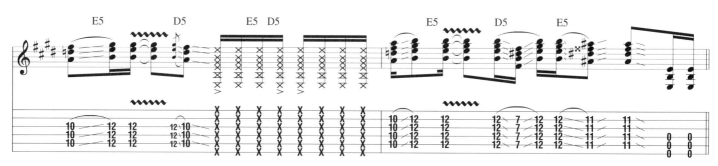

E5   D5   E5 D5   E5   D5   E5

Guitar Solo

Gtr. 2: w/ Rhy. Fig. 2, simile

D5 E5   D5   E5 D5   E5   D5   E5 D5

E5   D5   E5 D5   E5   D5   E5

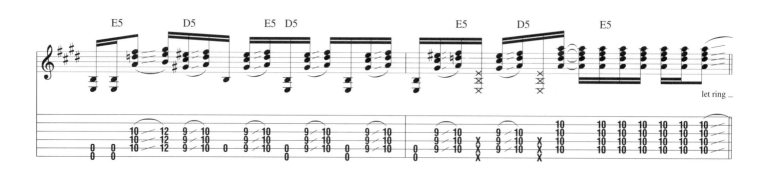

let ring __

78

80

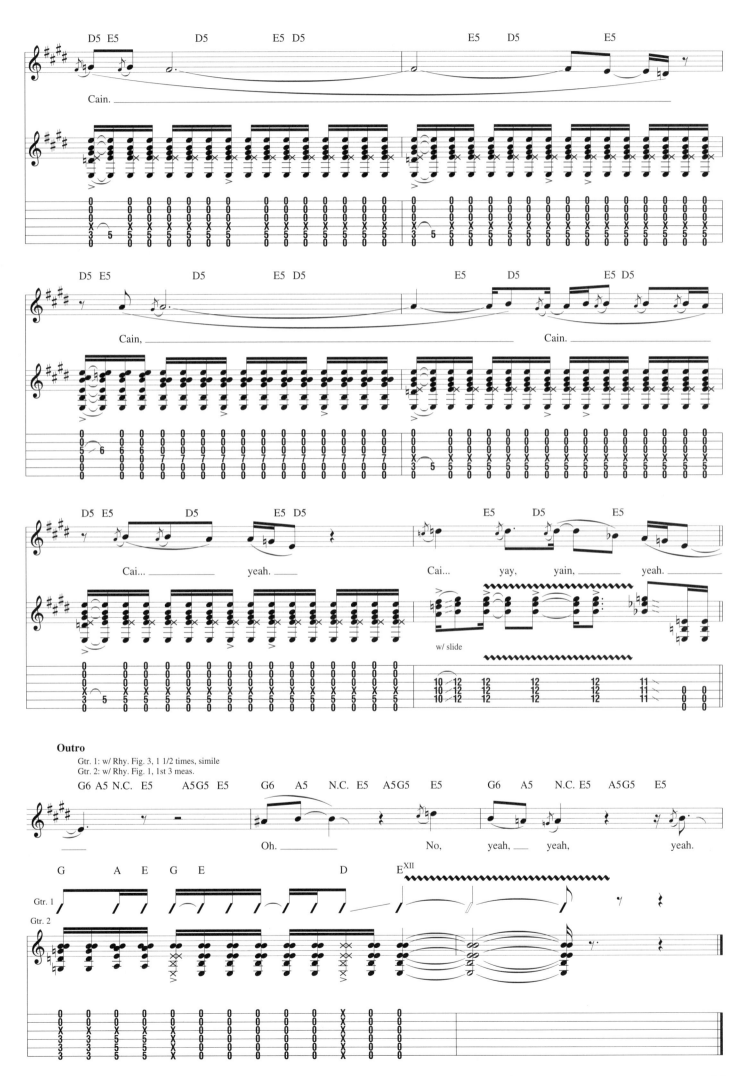

I Don't Want to Think About It

Words and Music by Ken Harrison

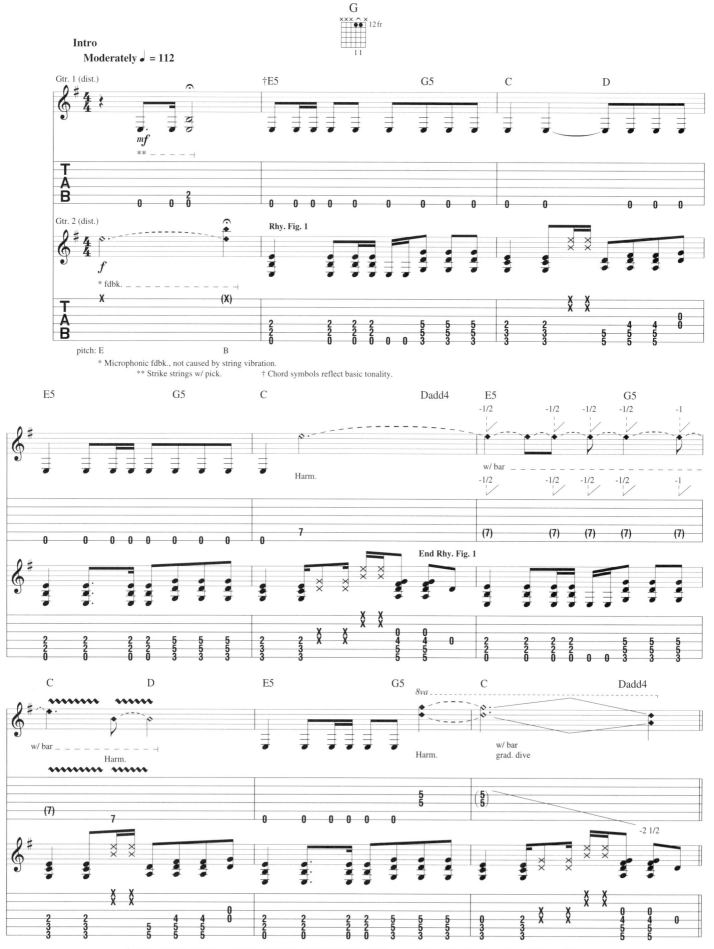

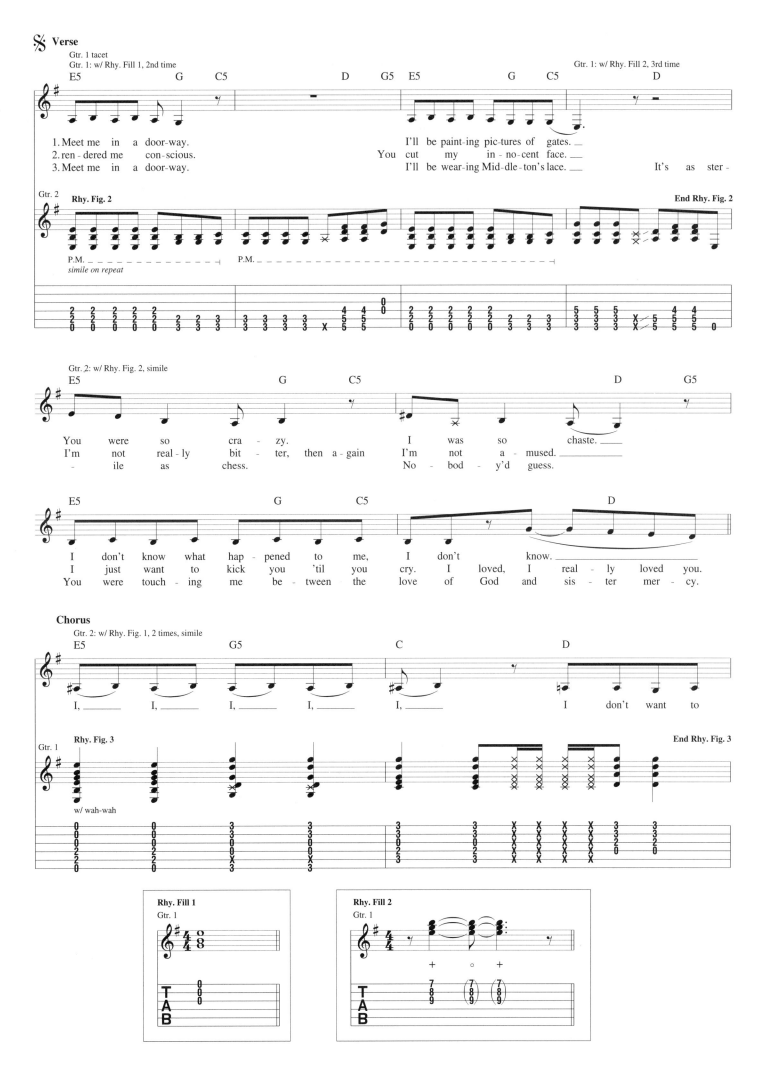

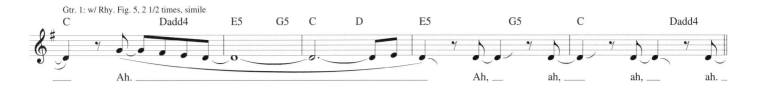

Outro

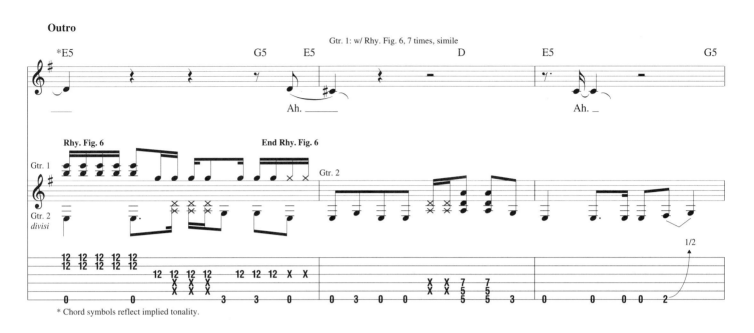

* Chord symbols reflect implied tonality.

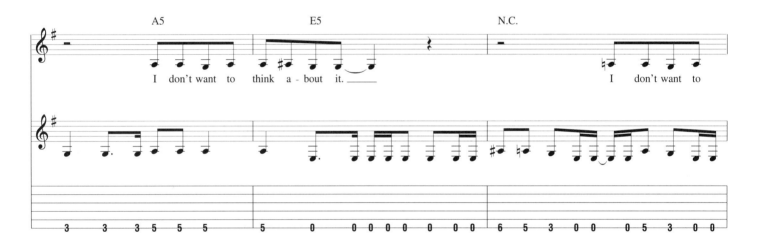

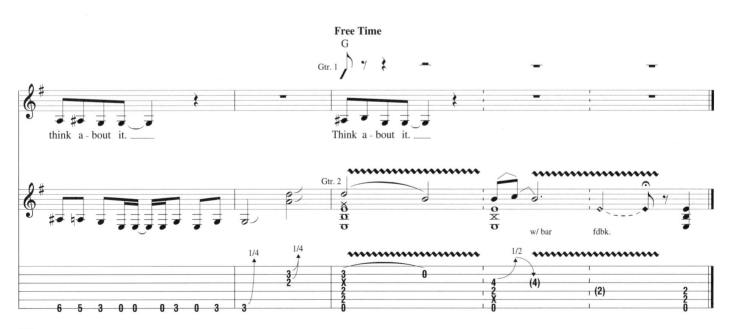

What Do You Hear in These Sounds

Words and Music by Dar Williams

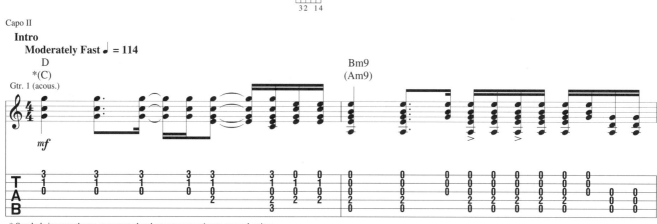

* Symbols in parentheses represent chord names respective to capoed guitar.
  Symbols above reflect actual sounding chord. Capoed fret is "0" in TAB.
  Chord symbols reflect basic tonality.

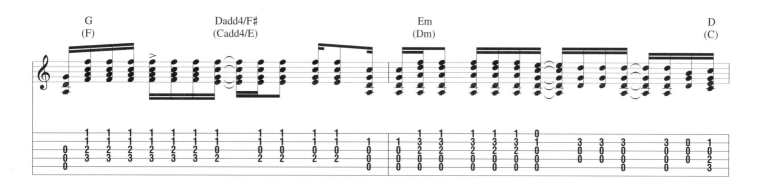

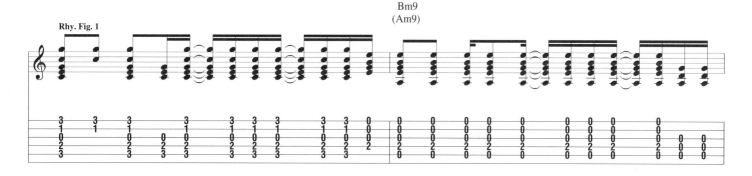

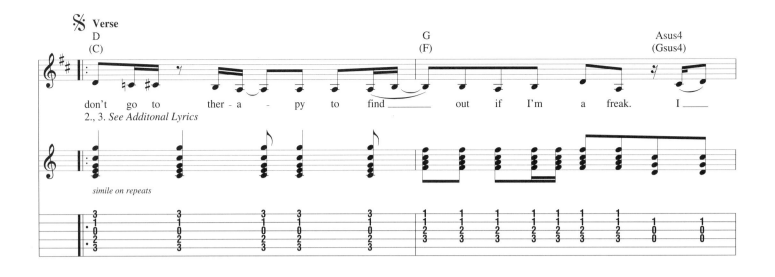

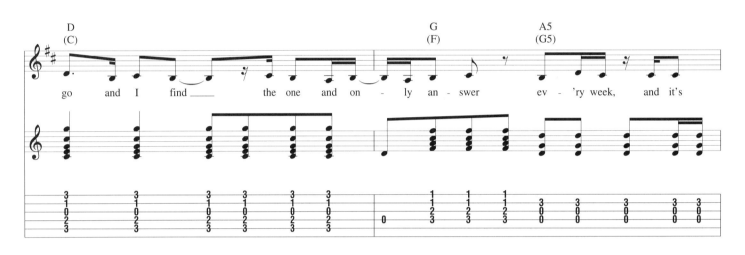

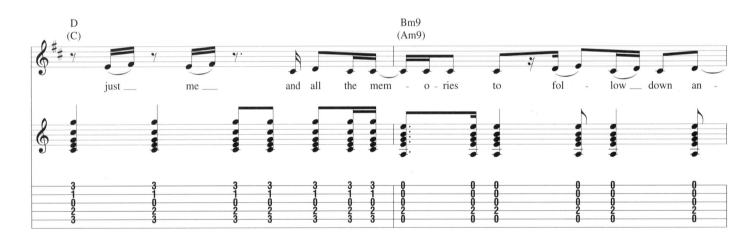

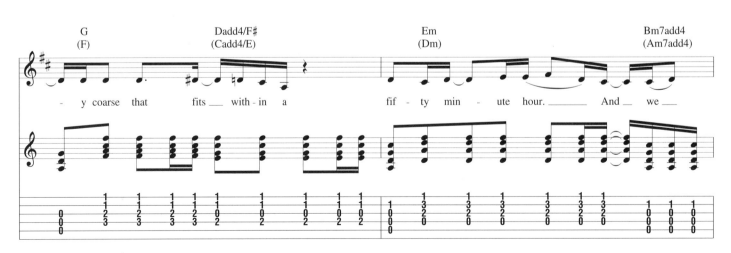

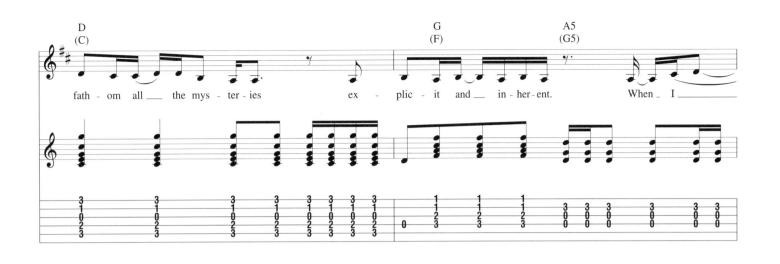

To Coda ⊕

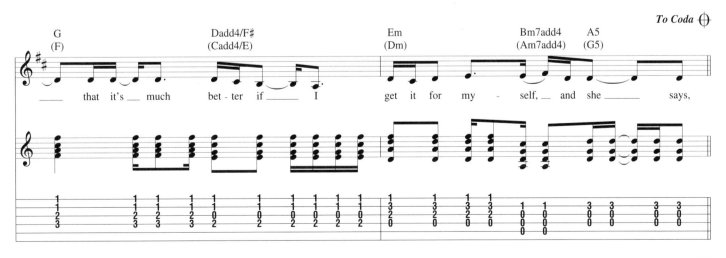

D.S. al Coda

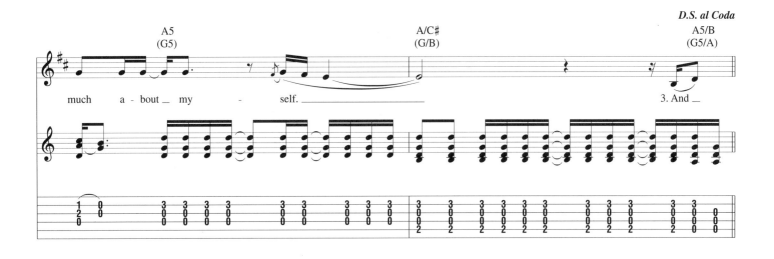

Coda

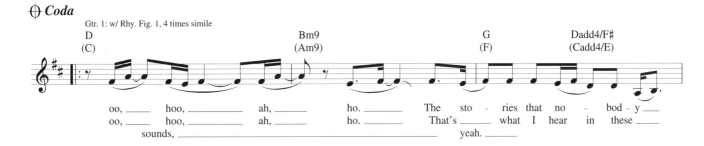

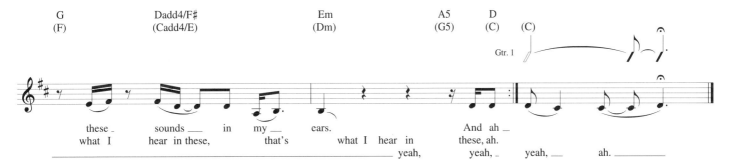

Additional Lyrics

2. I say I hear a doubt
   With the voice of true believing,
   And the promises to stay
   And the footsteps that are leaving.
   When she says, "Oh."
   I say, "What?" she says, " Exactly."
   I say, "What, you think I'm angry,
   Does that mean you think I'm angry?"
   She says, "Look, you come here every week
   With jigsaw pieces of your past.
   It's all on little soundbites
   And voices that are photographs
   And that's all yours, that's the guide,
   That's the map to tell me
   Where does the arrow point to."
   Who invented roses? And a...

3. And I wake up
   And I ask myself what state I'm in.
   And I say, "Well I'm lucky,
   'Cause I am like East Berlin."
   I had this wall
   And what I knew of the free world
   Was that I could see their fireworks
   And I could hear their radio.
   And I thought that ev'ry minute
   I would only start confessing.
   And they'd know that I was scared,
   They would know that I was guessing.
   But the wall came down
   And there they stood before me.
   But they're stumbling and they're mumbling
   And they're calling out just like me. And a...

Trouble

Words and Music by Tom Littlefield, Shawn Colvin and John Leventhal

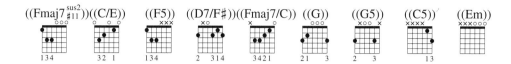

Gtr. 1: Capo I
Gtr. 2: Capo VIII

Intro
Moderately ♩ = 126

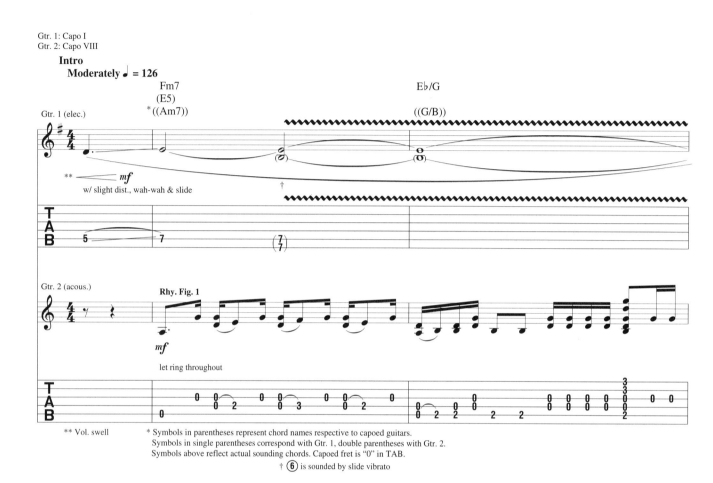

** Vol. swell * Symbols in parentheses represent chord names respective to capoed guitars.
Symbols in single parentheses correspond with Gtr. 1, double parentheses with Gtr. 2.
Symbols above reflect actual sounding chords. Capoed fret is "0" in TAB.

† ⑥ is sounded by slide vibrato

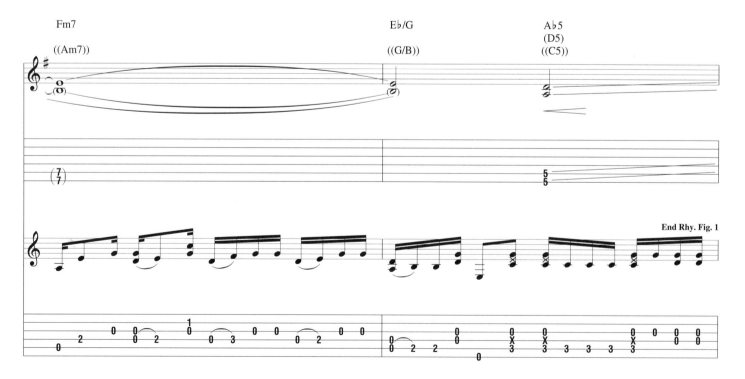

* ⑤ is sounded by slide vibrato

Verse

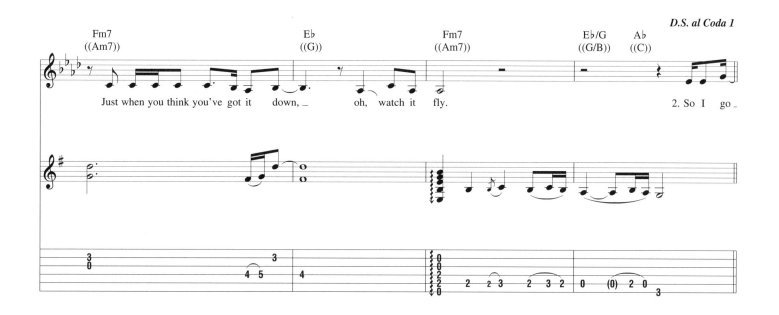

Just when you think you've got it down, _ oh, watch it fly. 2. So I go _

Coda 1

Guitar Solo

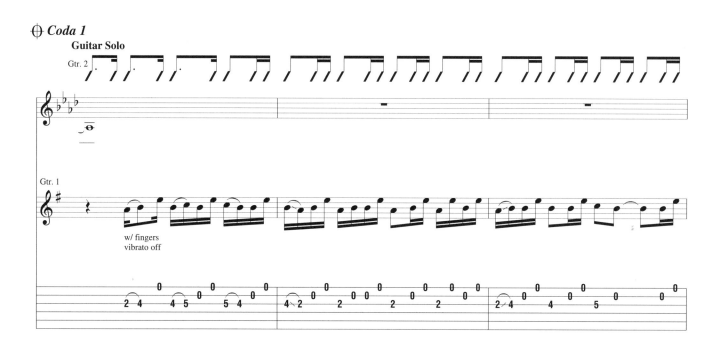

w/ fingers
vibrato off

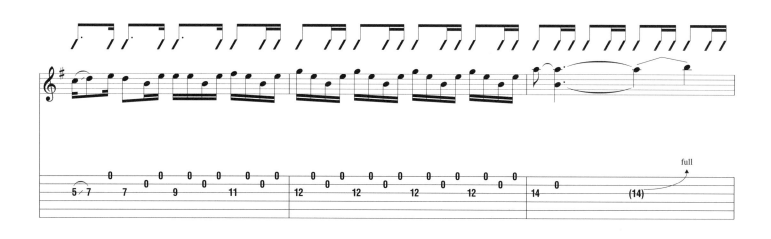

full

Additional Lyrics

Chorus 3. And I go to the trouble and I like it;
　　　　　That's where I'll be.
　　　　　Trouble is just like love;
　　　　　If it's half the way, then it's all I can see.

The One

Words and Music by Tracy Bonham

Read - y to _____ reach new lows, _____ dy - in' to _____ wash my hand.
Heav - en is _____ right out there, _____ leav - ing me _____ here be - hind.

End Riff A

Chorus

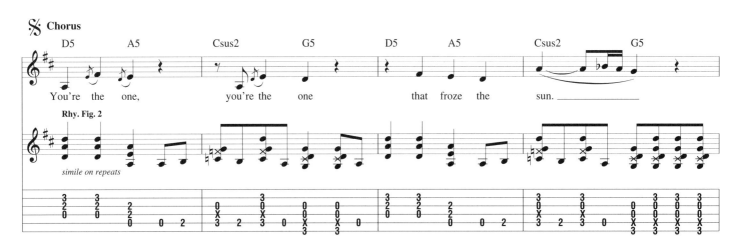

You're the one, you're the one that froze the sun. _____

Rhy. Fig. 2

simile on repeats

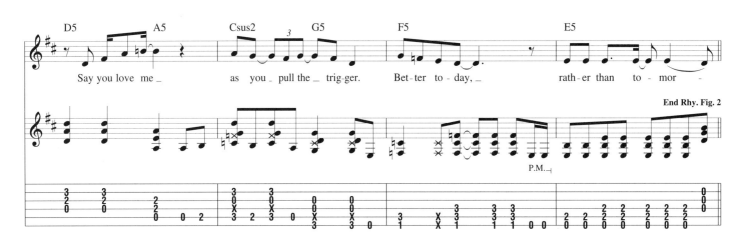

Say you love me ___ as you ___ pull the ___ trig - ger. Bet - ter to - day, ___ rath - er than to - mor -

End Rhy. Fig. 2

P.M.

1. Interlude

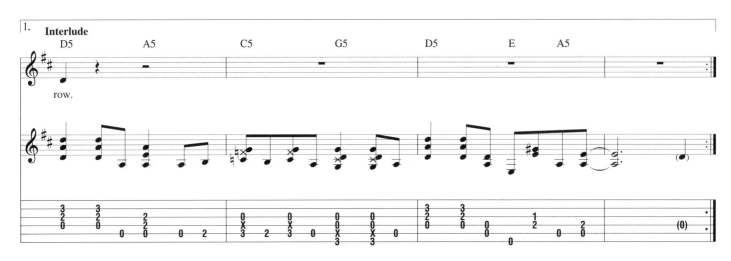

row.

Charm

**Words and Music by Angela McCluskey, Paul Cantelon, David "Shark" Shaw,
Thaddeus Corea, Scott Roewe, Tony Berg and Jon Brion**

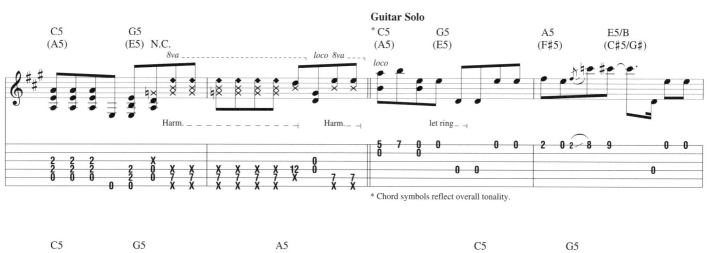

Guitar Solo

* Chord symbols reflect overall tonality.

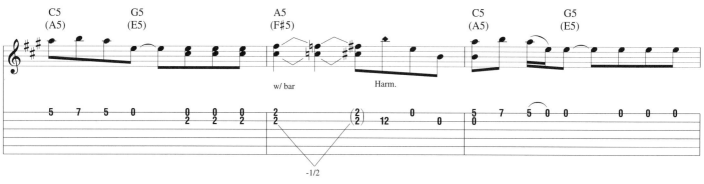

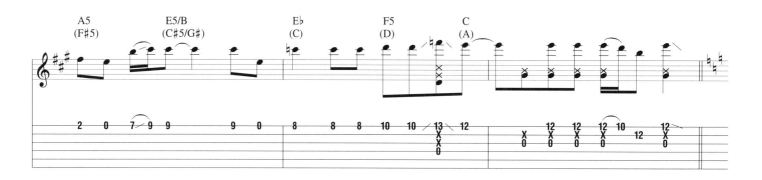

Bridge

Gtr. 1 tacet

It's my choice. ___

(Oh yeah.)

Save ___ my life. _____

* Chord symbols reflect implied tonality, next 5 measures.

D.S. al Coda

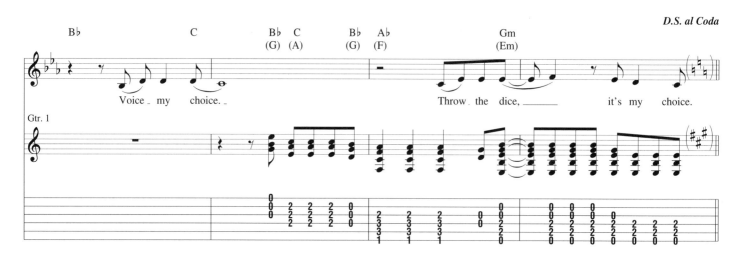

Voice ___ my choice. ___

Throw the dice, _____ it's my choice.

Gtr. 1

Hold Me Jordan

Words and Music by Tara MacLean

Gtr. 1: Capo II
Gtr. 2: Drop D Tuning; Capo IV:

① = E ④ = D
② = B ⑤ = A
③ = G ⑥ = D

Intro
Free Time

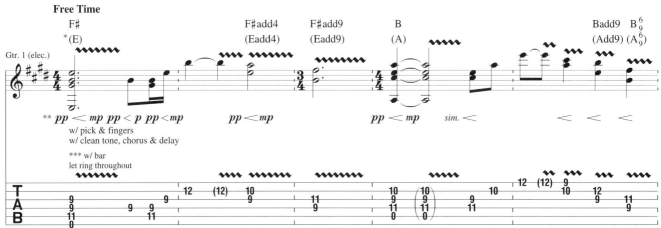

* Symbols in parentheses represent chord names respective to capoed guitar.
Symbols above reflect actual sounding chord. Capoed fret is "0" in TAB.
** w/ volume pedal throughout
*** next 10 meas.

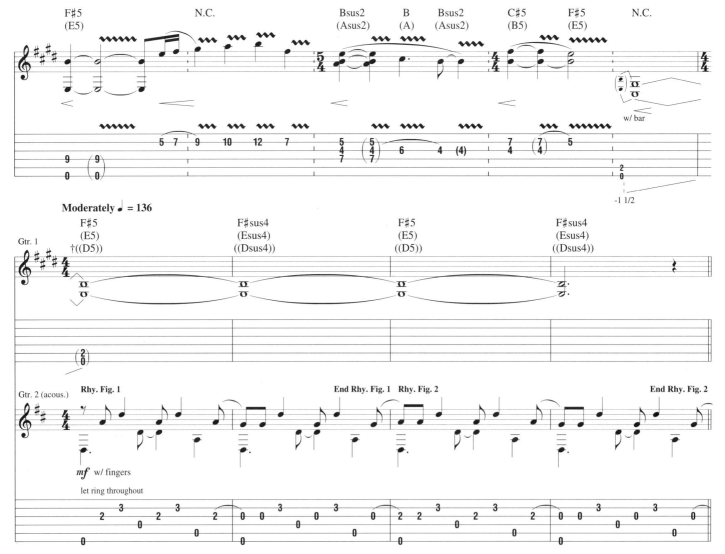

† Symbols in double parentheses represent chord names respective to Gtr. 2.
Capoed fret is "0" in TAB.

Periwinkle Sky

Words and Music by Victoria Williams

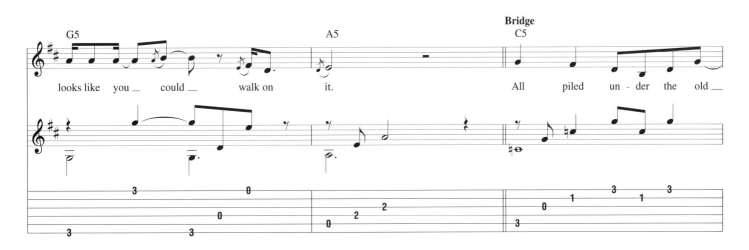

oak tree, ___ a cow told me, ___ "I think it's gon-na rain." A

cow ___ told me, ___ "Yeah, I ___ think it's gon - na rain." _____

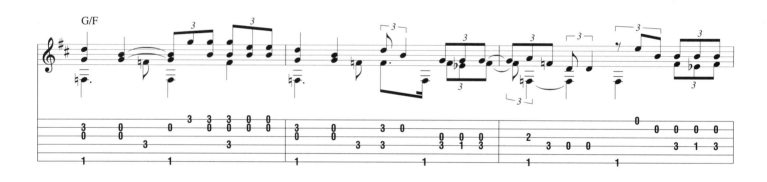

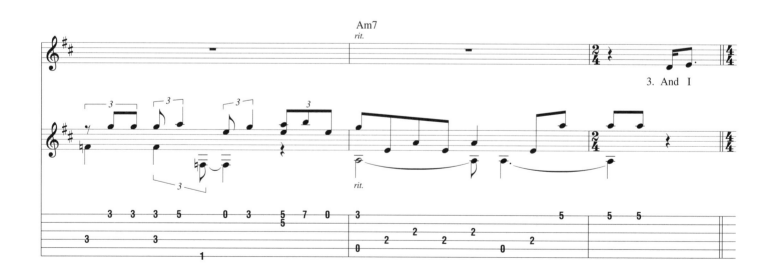

3. And I

Guitar Notation Legend

Guitar Music can be notated three different ways: on a *musical staff*, in *tablature*, and in *rhythm slashes*.

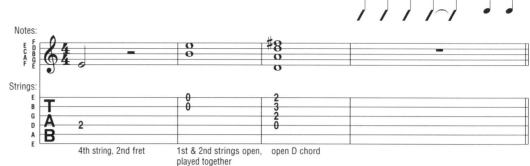

RHYTHM SLASHES are written above the staff. Strum chords in the rhythm indicated. Use the chord diagrams found at the top of the first page of the transcription for the appropriate chord voicings. Round noteheads indicate single notes.

THE MUSICAL STAFF shows pitches and rhythms and is divided by bar lines into measures. Pitches are named after the first seven letters of the alphabet.

TABLATURE graphically represents the guitar fingerboard. Each horizontal line represents a string, and each number represents a fret.

HALF-STEP BEND: Strike the note and bend up 1/2 step.

BEND AND RELEASE: Strike the note and bend up as indicated, then release back to the original note. Only the first note is struck.

HAMMER-ON: Strike the first (lower) note with one finger, then sound the higher note (on the same string) with another finger by fretting it without picking.

TRILL: Very rapidly alternate between the notes indicated by continuously hammering on and pulling off.

PICK SCRAPE: The edge of the pick is rubbed down (or up) the string, producing a scratchy sound.

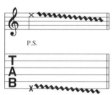

TREMOLO PICKING: The note is picked as rapidly and continuously as possible.

WHOLE-STEP BEND: Strike the note and bend up one step.

PRE-BEND: Bend the note as indicated, then strike it.

PULL-OFF: Place both fingers on the notes to be sounded. Strike the first note and without picking, pull the finger off to sound the second (lower) note.

TAPPING: Hammer ("tap") the fret indicated with the pick-hand index or middle finger and pull off to the note fretted by the fret hand.

MUFFLED STRINGS: A percussive sound is produced by laying the fret hand across the string(s) without depressing, and striking them with the pick hand.

VIBRATO BAR DIVE AND RETURN: The pitch of the note or chord is dropped a specified number of steps (in rhythm) then returned to the original pitch.

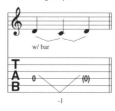

GRACE NOTE BEND: Strike the note and bend up as indicated. The first note does not take up any time.

VIBRATO: The string is vibrated by rapidly bending and releasing the note with the fretting hand.

LEGATO SLIDE: Strike the first note and then slide the same fret-hand finger up or down to the second note. The second note is not struck.

NATURAL HARMONIC: Strike the note while the fret-hand lightly touches the string directly over the fret indicated.

PALM MUTING: The note is partially muted by the pick hand lightly touching the string(s) just before the bridge.

VIBRATO BAR SCOOP: Depress the bar just before striking the note, then quickly release the bar.

SLIGHT (MICROTONE) BEND: Strike the note and bend up 1/4 step.

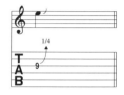

WIDE VIBRATO: The pitch is varied to a greater degree by vibrating with the fretting hand.

SHIFT SLIDE: Same as legato slide, except the second note is struck.

PINCH HARMONIC: The note is fretted normally and a harmonic is produced by adding the edge of the thumb or the tip of the index finger of the pick hand to the normal pick attack.

RAKE: Drag the pick across the strings indicated with a single motion.

VIBRATO BAR DIP: Strike the note and then immediately drop a specified number of steps, then release back to the original pitch.